GW00399968

WEST SUFFOLK COLLEGE LIBRARY
031033

SIR ROBERT WALPOLE

SIR ROBERT WALPOLE

BETTY KEMP

INTRODUCTION BY
A. J. P. TAYLOR

WEIDENFELD AND NICOLSON
LONDON

Designed by Behram Kapadia
for George Weidenfeld and Nicolson Ltd

ISBN 0 297 77067 5

Printed and bound in Great Britain by
Morrison & Gibb Ltd, London and Edinburgh

CONTENTS

ILLUSTRATIONS

between pages 86 and 87

INTRODUCTION

IN THE NINETEENTH CENTURY Sir Robert Walpole was credited with inventing the entire British constitution. Prime Minister, cabinet government, supremacy of the House of Commons, and the two-party system were all unknown when he became First Lord of the Treasury in 1721, and were, it was thought, all fully grown when he left office twenty-one years later. We do not believe much of that any longer. In Walpole's time the cabinet did not govern as a united body; the House of Commons was not supreme; there was no two-party system.

But one thing cannot be taken away from Walpole: he was just as much the first modern Prime Minister we should recognize as Adam was the first man. He tied together Crown and Commons as no minister had done before. He sounded like a modern Prime Minister even though some sources of his power were different. There had been many great parliamentary figures before Walpole's time, but he was the first who could have made sense of a present-day parliament after a little experience. He took the venom out of politics and ended the era when men ruined or killed each other for political reasons. Experience had made him tolerant on principle, and he showed no resentment even against bitter and unfair opponents. Despite his lack of a party machine, he was the greatest of parliamentary managers. Opinions differ, but in my view there is no doubt that he used means of influence which would now be regarded as corrupt. However such means were the common fashion of his time, and it is thanks to Walpole that British politics are still comparatively civilized. He would, however, have been surprised to know that the principal memorial to him is his collection of pictures, now in the Hermitage Gallery in Leningrad.

A. J. P. TAYLOR

HAPPY WOULD IT BE for any Country, especially a free one (such as we call ours) if no Servant of the Crown had Authority beyond the proper Bounds of his own office. But even if we could suppose a Series of great Monarchs, equally capable and vigilant with our present most gracious Sovereign, it would hardly be possible but that superior Abilities, longer Experience, fairer Pretensions, a Mastery in Expedients, a larger Interest in Family or Friends, the personal Affection of his Prince; it is hardly possible, I say, but that one or more of these would add to the Weight of some particular Officer, and lift him into that mighty Individual, a Prime Minister. Since we must not expect, therefore, to remain long without some such Weight upon our Shoulders, let us study how to make it sit as easy, and shift it as often, as we can possibly.

JAMES RALPH: *A Critical History of the Administration of Sir Robert Walpole* 1743

I

A PRIME MINISTER?

ROBERT WALPOLE was a Prime Minister before Prime Ministers were a regular part of British political life; when they were occasional, suspect things, Kings' favourites, an exception to a rule. The rule was that all the King's ministers were equally his servants, each of them responsible directly to the King for his own department. No rule was broken when 'prime' was used simply as an adjective; if it was so used, the prime ministers were the ministers who held the great offices of state.

In the early eighteenth century, however, 'Prime Minister' was coming to be commonly used as a noun. It was used to describe a minister who had obtained more than his due share of the King's favour and could, in consequence, lord it over his colleagues. It did not matter what office that minister held. There was no office of 'Prime Minister', nor was there any idea that the title went with any particular office. 'Prime Minister' was a tribute to a man – to a minister, not to his office. But it was a reluctant tribute and most people believed that the less often it was heard, the better for the health of the constitution. The difference between the two kinds of Prime Minister, one good and one bad, was clear enough to contemporaries. 'According to our Constitution', said Samuel Sandys, one of Walpole's most persistent detractors, in 1741, 'we can have no sole and prime Minister: We ought always to have several prime Ministers or Officers of State: Every such Officer has his proper Department; and no Officer ought to meddle in the Affairs belonging to the Department of another.'

To ask whether Walpole was the first Prime Minister, as people often do, is to use 'Prime Minister' as a noun. Even so, it is a tricky question. The answer depends on who asks the question, and when. What people meant by a Prime Minister in Walpole's time is quite different from what they meant a century later. This again is different from what we mean today, though the difference is less. From the 1820s or 1830s, there was a recognized and accepted position of Prime Minister; from 1867, the Prime Minister was normally the leader of the party which had just won a general election. We are therefore faced not with one question, but with two. Was Walpole a Prime Minister in the sense in which his contemporaries understood the words? Was he a Prime Minister in the sense in which the nineteenth century understood the words?

The first question is easy to answer. Walpole was a Prime Minister in his own time because his contemporaries called him 'a Prime Minister'. They did not do this because the office he held, First Lord of the Treasury, was one of the great offices of state. They were not using 'prime' as an adjective, but 'Prime Minister' as a noun. They did this because Walpole seemed to be personally more important and more powerful than the other ministers, and to have a monopoly of the King's favour and confidence. This is what a 'Prime Minister' meant to Walpole's contemporaries. This explains why the Earl of Sunderland in 1721, and the Earl of Bute in 1760, who both held the court post of Groom of the Stole – not an office of state at all – could yet be called Prime Minister. Walpole's contemporaries were aware that there were prime ministers in other countries and that in some, France for example, there was an office of 'Prime Minister'. But in England the office did not exist, and the position was not supposed to. Therefore those of Walpole's contemporaries who called him a Prime Minister were criticizing him, believing him to occupy a position which ought not to exist. 'Sole Minister', 'Grand Vizier', 'King's Favourite', were synonyms for 'Prime Minister', as was the longer definition offered by *The Craftsman*, a journal founded in 1726 by Bolingbroke, one of Walpole's fiercest critics: 'an arbitrary Viceroy or deputy Tyrant ... inconsistent with the nature of a free State'.

Walpole was not the first to be called a 'Prime Minister', but certainly it was not an old term when it was applied to him. It seems indeed to be an early eighteenth-century one, hardly found before Walpole's political life began. Being a 'Prime Minister' was one of the charges against Edward Harley, Earl of Oxford, when he was impeached in 1715. The title was also applied retrospectively to former favourites who seemed to merit it. In 1706, a book was published entitled *The Secret Memoirs of Robert Dudley, Earl of Leicester, Prime Minister and Favourite of Queen Elizabeth.* It was matched in 1740 by *The Life and Death of Pierce Gaveston, grand Favourite and Prime Minister to that unfortunate Prince, Edward II.*

Just as Walpole was not the first to be called Prime Minister, so he was not the first of a series of Prime Ministers. He was called a Prime Minister for more than ten years – from soon after 1730 until he resigned in 1742. This long span did not make Englishmen any fonder of the phenomenon. 'No more Prime Ministers' was the hope in 1742. Politicians, and those whom one might have expected to want the title themselves, shared this dislike of Prime Ministers. George Grenville, First Lord of the Treasury in 1763, was not old-fashioned when, in 1761, he spoke of the 'odious title' of Prime Minister. Lord North, in the 1770s, would not allow his family, even in private, to call him a Prime Minister. For more than another half century after Walpole's death, there was only one question that Englishmen could ask about Prime Ministers – 'Is there a Prime Minister?' The question '*Who* is the Prime Minister?' would not have made sense. It could not be asked until there always was one, and no one disputed that there should be.

By the middle of the nineteenth century, this change had taken place. As a corollary, Prime Minister had a new meaning. It was defined, for example, as the chief of a cabinet enjoying the support of both Houses of Parliament, but especially of the House of Commons. The cabinet could, at this stage, be defined too. It had come to be a body of ministers who came and went at the same time and were chosen by the Prime Minister, though not of course without reference to the monarch. The fact that in the late 1840s Lord John Russell was criticized for being a 'weak' Prime Minister, not able to control his colleagues, is a measure of the change in opinion which underlay the change in fact. Prime Ministers were no longer odious and they were expected to control their colleagues. The mid-nineteenth century, looking back and believing that it saw in Walpole much that was comparable with its own Prime Ministers, began to call him 'the first Prime Minister'.

We do not need, here, to pronounce them right or wrong. But they *were* wrong, in many ways. For example, Walpole did not practise cabinet government as it was practised in the middle of the nineteenth century. It would not be unreasonable to say that Walpole controlled his colleagues better than Russell did his; although the comparison is not very meaningful, because the situation was so different. Walpole's colleagues were not appointed at the same time as himself and there was no suggestion that they ought to resign at the same time. In fact, none did resign and, apart from Walpole, there was only one important ministerial change when he went out of office in 1742.

Walpole's contemporaries did not call him the first Prime Minister, nor did they even imply that he was the first. Indeed, they implied the exact opposite. Authors of pamphlets and prints glanced over their shoulders at Edward II and Richard II, Kings who lost their thrones because they listened to bad advice from favourites; they cited Queen Elizabeth's Leicester, James I's Buckingham and perhaps, more recently, Clarendon, Danby and Harley. These were the 'overgrown ministers', the 'excrescences on the constitution', who monopolized the King's favour, pushing him towards a policy designed to further their own ends, or a particular interest, not the interest of the nation as a whole.

In fact, Walpole became a Prime Minister firstly because of his ascendancy in the commons, and only secondly because of the King's favour. This was the other way round from William Cecil, Elizabeth I's great minister, to whom Walpole's contemporaries sometimes compared him. His position would have been less remarkable, and his task easier, if he had repeated Cecil's role, that of a Prime Minister sent by the monarch to manage the Commons.

But there was one contemporary charge against Prime Ministers which, at first sight, seems as if it might be new, as it recognized a difference between an eighteenth-century Prime Minister and earlier ones; this was the charge that a Prime Minister was incompatible with the balance of the constitution. This charge, implying as it did that Prime Ministers were corrupters of parliaments or of the House of Commons, destroyers of the independence on which the balance of the constitution was built, seems new because the balance of the constitution is commonly associated with the settlement after the Glorious Revolution of 1688. Yet those who used this apparently new eighteenth-century argument also believed that the constitution and its balance were older than 1689, and wished to return to the 'ancient constitution'.

They believed that an eighteenth-century Prime Minister had at his disposal new methods of corruption, but still they did not see him as a new phenomenon.

So although many of Walpole's contemporary critics bracketed him with Edward II's 'minions' and James I's 'favourites', there were, in fact, many new things about Walpole's position, the most important being his relationship to the House of Commons. This relationship is so striking that nowadays we tend to think of it as part of the definition of Walpole as a Prime Minister. Contemporaries did not do this; to them, Walpole's ascendancy in the House of Commons was not new in kind, though it may have been new in extent. What *was* new in kind was a Prime Minister who was the leading member of the House of Commons.

This linking of the House of Commons with the King's government was not only new, but of great importance historically. During the whole of the period that Walpole was known as Prime Minister, nearly all the other ministers were members of the House of Lords – the House of Lords in those days being the place where ministers sat. The new relationship between the government and the House of Commons was therefore effected not by the ministers as a whole but by Walpole himself, together with some others holding lesser office: for example, Under-Secretaries of State and, in the legal sphere, the Attorney and Solicitor-General.

Thus there was no precedent for a Prime Minister in the House of Commons; until then, a 'Great Man', as Walpole became known after the mid-1720s, was expected sooner or later to be created a peer and moved up to the House of Lords – this had happened to Harley, Stanhope and many more of Walpole's contemporaries. A peerage was considered to be a political promotion, not simply a social elevation; and prominence in the Commons was usually rewarded by promotion to the Lords.

Walpole's rejection of this well-worn traditional path was quite new and quite deliberate, and his remaining – for twenty years – a 'Great Man', and not a great lord, transformed political life.

Walpole was born on 26 August 1676, sixteen years after the Restoration of Charles II and three years before the Exclusion Crisis – the attempt to exclude James, Duke of York, from the succession to the throne. It was about that time that the words 'Whig' and 'Tory' first became widely used in politics. When Shaftesbury, 'the first Whig', died and Russell and Sidney, the first Whig martyrs, were executed, Walpole was seven; at the time of the Glorious Revolution, he was twelve.

Walpole was the third son of a middling Norfolk squire, a prudent and improving farmer and something of a scholar. The Walpole family was rooted in Norfolk: generation after generation had married into other Norfolk families. They had produced a number of members of parliament, but no prominent ones. Walpole's grandfather sat in the Convention Parliament which restored Charles II in 1660, and his father, a Whig, sat in all William III's parliaments from 1689 until his death in 1700.

As the third son, Walpole could not expect a political career. He was educated first at a small school at Great Dunham and then at Eton and Cambridge. There was some idea of a career in the Church for him; but the deaths of his two elder brothers changed the family situation, forcing Walpole to leave Cambridge after two years, in 1698, to learn farming and help his father manage the estate. The earliest surviving letter of Walpole's is the one he wrote to the Provost of King's College, resigning his scholarship. It is dated 19 May 1698.

Walpole's father, often quoted for his ambition to make his son 'the first grazier in the county', should be remembered for more than this. His university career, like his son's, had been cut short, and for the same reason. His father died in 1667, his mother soon afterwards; he was therefore left, at the age of seventeen, to manage the estate and look after his younger brothers and sisters. At Cambridge he was known as an earnest, scholarly young man, with a capacity and a disposition for hard work. Family responsibilities strengthened these characteristics. He kept meticulous accounts, rigorously controlled all household expenditure, and spent nothing on frivolity or fashion. (He did, however, indulge his taste for serious reading, building up and leaving to his son a library packed with editions of Latin and Greek authors and solid volumes of history, law and theology.) He prospered by hard work, strict household economy, and the use of new Dutch methods of husbandry: soil improvement, the cultivation of turnips and clover, the rotation of crops. He enclosed land and applied the new methods to it. By the 1680s, he had paid off his debts and saved money. In 1689, he was elected Member of Parliament for King's Lynn. In 1697, he enlarged his property by buying a valuable neighbouring estate. To do this, he had to raise mortgages; unfortunately, when he died in November 1700, aged only fifty, his mortgages had not been paid off, and they were a heavy addition to the responsibilities he left to his son.

Walpole reversed his father's order of priorities. Politics came first, his financial situation second: he did not wait to pay off his debts, but stood for parliament as soon as his father died. Nor did he live frugally. He was newly married, too, and his wife was extravagant. She was Catherine Shorter, daughter of a Baltic timber merchant from Kent, and granddaughter of a Lord Mayor of London. Walpole's father had arranged the marriage in 1699 and it took place in the summer of 1700. This departure from the usual pattern of Walpole marriages – with other Norfolk or Suffolk families – was no doubt partly a reflection of Walpole's father's progress from successful Norfolk estate management to the London world of politics. Nevertheless, it remains a slightly surprising departure.

Both Walpole and his wife wanted to be in London – he for the political world, she for the social world – and they lived at first with Catherine's grandmother, widow of Sir Erasmus Philipps. In 1705, when Walpole's financial position was a little easier, he bought a house in Arlington Street – this was to be their London home for the next ten years.

They were, it was said, 'the handsomest couple in London' – he sociable and unaffected, she dark and romantic; though it soon appeared that she was also petulant, jealous and rather foolish. They had four surviving children, three sons, Robert, Edward and Horace, and one daughter, Mary; a daughter, Catherine, and a son, William, died in infancy. The youngest child, Horace, was born in 1717 and called after his uncle Horatio, Walpole's younger brother. In 1715, the Walpoles moved to a larger house in Arlington Street; although, by this time, the marriage had broken down. Catherine was emotional, unbalanced, liable to engage in amorous adventures; she remained hopelessly extravagant. But the couple continued to live together, Walpole remaining kind and patient with Catherine's vagaries, until her death in the summer of 1737.

Six months later Walpole married again, and very happily. His second wife was Maria Skerrett, with whom he had been intimate for perhaps fourteen years, and who had been living since 1725 at Old Lodge, Richmond Park, which Walpole had had rebuilt and furnished for her. Their daughter, Mary, too, born in 1725, was now able to join the Walpole household. Maria was a woman of wit, charm and generosity. She was thirty-five when she married Walpole. She had been for many years – since about 1720 – the close friend of Lady Mary Wortley Montagu, most celebrated of eighteenth-century literary ladies, who had her to stay with her in Twickenham and London. Lady Mary, who declared 'dear Molly Skerrett' to be 'in the first rank of her friends', vouched for her intelligence and good judgement. 'Everyone', said Sir Thomas

Robinson, 'gives her a good character both as to her understanding and good nature'. Her portrait suggests she was serious-minded, competent and composed, with a streak of humour but no coquettishness. John, Lord Hervey, Lady Mary's rival in wit, and Walpole's supporter, described her as intelligent, agreeable, and 'very pretty'. He told Walpole that 'what Miss Skerrett said of people was of importance to every man in England' because of her relationship with Walpole. But neither Hervey nor anyone else seriously suggested either that Maria had any power in politics or any influence over Walpole's decisions – or that she wished for this. Walpole must have found her an intelligent and interested companion, and clearly he loved her deeply. 'His happiness', said his brother Horatio, was 'very deservedly wrapt up in her.' But their relationship, though quite open, was discreet. It remains private. There are no surviving letters between Walpole and Maria – perhaps there never were any. Only one letter, in fact, survives between Walpole and his first wife, and nearly all the papers that would tell us about Walpole's early life have been lost or destroyed. Sadly, Maria died in childbirth only a few months after their marriage.

Walpole, then, inherited from his father a valuable and improved estate (although with some mortgages) and perhaps, also, he inherited his father's determination and capacity for hard work. But in temperament, 'benevolent, good-humoured' Walpole, as his son called him, was not like either of his parents. His mother seems to have been a somewhat harsh, complaining woman. She lived until 1711, when Walpole was thirty-five, and seems not to have exercised any great influence on her children, either before or after her husband's death. There is no evidence that she took any interest in Walpole's career. Walpole was generous and affectionate to his brother and three sisters – as he was to his own children – and took pains to help them. He and his brother Horatio, two years his junior, were friends and associates throughout Walpole's life; his favourite sister, the impulsive and warm-hearted Dolly, owed much to him, including her happy marriage, in 1713, to his friend and colleague, Charles Viscount Townshend of Raynham in Norfolk. The marriage linked two influential Norfolk families, and cemented a personal and political alliance between Walpole and Townshend which lasted for many years.

After his father's death in November 1700, Walpole succeeded him in January 1701 as Member of Parliament for Castle Rising; he sat for this borough in the two short parliaments at the end of William III's reign (February to November 1701, and December 1701 to July 1702). In August 1702, at the general election following William's death, Walpole was elected for King's Lynn. He represented it for the next forty years, spanning the five parliaments of Anne's reign, the two of George I's, and the first two of George II's.

Walpole held three minor administrative offices in Anne's reign, between 1705 and 1710. These gave him responsibility and a knowledge of war finance; they also brought him into contact with Marlborough and Godolphin, Anne's great ministers, and with the Queen herself. By the end of Anne's reign he was known as a firm Whig, an excellent administrator, and a man of great parliamentary talents. He was outstanding in the House of Commons, an able debater, quick to grasp the essential points in an argument and to rescue, for his audience, principles from detail. He was clear-headed, cool and cheerful. He seemed in fact marked out for great advancement in George I's reign, with the inevitable change from Tory to Whig predominance.

It is therefore surprising (and it was surprising to contemporaries too) that the first seven years of George I's reign did not bring a straightforward promotion of a promising Whig career. Walpole was appointed Paymaster of the Forces in 1714, held one of the great offices of state, First Lord of the Treasury, for eighteen months and then, for three years, from 1717 to 1720, was out of office and in opposition to the Whig ministers he had left. In 1720, when he was appointed Paymaster again, his position seemed less secure than it had done at the beginning of the reign. In 1721, he again reached the office of First Lord of the Treasury, and this time he kept it for twenty-one years.

He was not called a Prime Minister yet. This came in the 1730s, and with it came opposition. Much of it was opposition not to what Walpole was doing, but to what he was, or was supposed to be – opposition to his unconstitutional position. A lot of it was so rancorous, wrong-headed, and, apparently, deliberately falsifying that it is astonishing to find Walpole's reactions so reasonable, so unflurried and, until the very end, so good-tempered. Yet perhaps, on reflection, it is possible to see why. Walpole's temperament explains a good deal; his convictions explain the rest. He was as convinced as his opponents were of the importance of the argument; he was as deeply concerned as they were for the constitution; and perhaps he never quite despaired of trying to make them realize this.

Although it is not easy for us to be as good-tempered and patient with Walpole's opponents as he was himself, it is important to try, and not simply to discount their endless talk about the constitution as hypocrisy, their way of making respectable their dislike of Walpole's policy or his person. Their passion for the constitution, however foreign to us, was quite genuine and not even strange. It was not based simply on fear, though there was plenty of that – after all, even in the 1730s, the Glorious Revolution had happened in the lifetime of everyone over forty. Their opposition to Walpole stemmed from an absolute conviction – a conviction that the whole way of life and welfare of a state was positively determined by the kind of constitution it had.

2

PRELUDE
1701–21

WALPOLE sat in the House of Commons for forty-one years, from January 1701 to February 1742. His appointment as First Lord of the Treasury for the second time, in April 1721, divides his parliamentary career almost exactly in half. He held the office for nearly twenty-one years, until he resigned in February 1742. Thus the first twenty years of his parliamentary career may be considered as a prelude to the last twenty-one. They are not the only 'prelude' in Walpole's career; at least two alternatives can be posited. These would have regard to Walpole's stature rather than to his office, and would justify this on the grounds that the office he held does not explain his domination of the political scene in the 1720s and 1730s.

The first alternative might be called 'prelude to the Great Man' and would end soon after 1722, when Sunderland died, and Walpole and Townshend were left as the two leading members of the government, or perhaps in 1724, when Carteret, leader of Sunderland's group after his death, failed to oust Townshend. In the mid-1720s, Walpole was beginning to be called the Great Man, though Townshend never regarded him as an equal, let alone a superior. The second alternative might be called 'prelude to a Prime Minister'. This would end somewhere about 1730, when

Townshend resigned. After this Walpole is commonly described as 'the Minister' or 'a Prime or Sole Minister'.

These alternative preludes are, in a sense, as real as the one ending with Walpole's appointment to the Treasury in 1721. They are, however, less tangible, and the attempt to date and define them is distracting. Perhaps, too, they distort the picture: it is not always helpful to search too hard for the end of a man's development in its beginning.

For, to Walpole's contemporaries, there was nothing in the first half of his career that made his later domination inevitable, or even likely. This was because it was a new kind of domination, not because they in any way doubted his abilities. They respected his administrative competence, admired his handling of public finance, and recognized his mastery in the Commons. He explained financial matters simply and clearly, by cutting through non-essentials. He spoke often, fluently and effectively, sometimes eloquently, arguing his case with assurance and good temper. It is true that the combination of these skills was to be the basis of his later domination of both the House of Commons and the government; but in the first half of Walpole's career such a form of double domination was not guessed at. His skills were much more likely to lead him, perhaps as First Lord of the Treasury, to the House of Lords, which was still thought of as the centre of government. This was the path which had been taken by Godolphin, also called a Prime Minister and, like Walpole, outstanding as a successful practitioner of new financial techniques. Harley went the same way. Nearly all Walpole's ministerial colleagues were in the House of Lords throughout his career. In 1714, Walpole and Stanhope were amongst the very few prominent Whig politicians who were not peers – by creation even if not by birth – and Stanhope himself was created a peer in 1717.

Revolution Whig 1701–14

There was never any doubt that Walpole was a Whig, though right from the beginning many of his aims and policies went beyond party. However, the word 'Whig' had necessarily a different meaning in Anne's reign from its meaning in 1679–81, when the label was pinned to Shaftesbury's Country Party. Bolingbroke, looking back from the 1730s, was going to argue that the 1688 Revolution, by achieving many of the aims of the so-called Whigs or Country Party, had destroyed the *raison d'être* of both labels: Whig and Tory.

These were Bolingbroke's later reflections, not apparent to him, or to others, in Anne's reign. If William III's reign was a period of some confusion of parties, with a King who was not a party man, Anne's reign was a time of renewed party strife, with a Queen who had definite Tory sympathies. 'Whig' and 'Tory' had been clear-cut divisions at the time of the Exclusion Crisis. In 1680, Whigs stood for the exclusion of James, Duke of York, from the throne on the grounds that he was a Catholic; they stood for a King limited by parliament, and owing his title to parliament, not a King by divine right; they stood for a King who should be allied with Protestant Holland in place of a King who was allied with, and indeed a pensioner of, Louis XIV; they stood for toleration to Protestants of all kinds. If the Exclusionists had won, Charles II's successor would have been a Whig King and the Tory doctrines of divine right and passive obedience would have been clearly defeated.

They did not win, however, and James II succeeded to the throne in 1685. The Revolution which turned him out in December 1688 was not a Whig Revolution but a national Revolution, engineered by a coalition of Whigs and Tories. The position was therefore not so clear in 1689 as it would have been if James had been kept from the throne instead of being turned off it. Naturally, the Whigs felt that their doctrines had been vindicated. Nevertheless, in the Declaration of Rights, one of the most important of their doctrines was modified, specifically in order not to alienate Tory supporters of the Revolution. This was the basic doctrine of the right to the throne. The Whigs held that James's subjects had resisted and deposed him because he had infringed the conditions on which he held the throne, the fundamental laws of the kingdom and, in particular, the contract between King and subjects which bound them to obey him and him to rule them well. The Declaration of Rights listed the ways in which James had broken the fundamental laws of the kingdom, but, after long debates in both Houses, the question of why the throne was vacant was simply answered, or evaded, by the statement that James had abdicated.

In terms of personnel, too, this Revolution was not a Whig victory. William III had a hereditary claim to the throne, though he had not succeeded to the throne by virtue of it. By hereditary right, through his mother who was Charles II's sister, William was next in succession to Anne. He did not regard himself as a monarch tied to the Whigs either by gratitude or by sympathy, and he had no preference for Whig over Tory ministers.

In the 1690s, parties were deplored as well as being confused: divisions were considered unpatriotic and unnecessary. Party warfare weakened the national response to the national danger – the French threat to the balance of Europe, to English liberties and to the Protestant succession. Parties had been born of opposition to a tyrant King. The need for them had passed with his banishment and with the securing of certain rights invaded or threatened by him. William III's speech at the opening of his last parliament in December 1701 expressed a view of parties which was not unique to him:

Let me conjure you to disappoint the only Hopes of our Enemies, by your Unanimity . . . lay aside all Parties and Divisions; let there be no other Distinction heard of among us for the Future, but of those who are for the Protestant Religion, and the present Establishment, and of those who mean a Popish Prince and a French Government . . . see England hold the Balance of Europe, and to be indeed at the head of the Protestant interest.

So William was a Revolution monarch, but not a Whig monarch. The principles which had divided Whigs and Tories in the 1680s were less relevant in the 1690s, and would perhaps have died if William and Mary had founded a dynasty; but they had no children. Anne (younger daughter of James II's first marriage), was also a Revolution monarch, as much so, she once said, as William, but she came close to appearing a Tory monarch. James II died in 1701, so that Anne was, by that accident, closer to the hereditary succession than William or even Mary (elder daughter of James II's first marriage) had been. She sympathized with some Tory principles, especially High Church principles. Moreover the Duke of Gloucester, the only one of her children to survive infancy, died in 1700, before she came to the throne. In spite of the Act of Settlement, therefore, the Protestant succession was uncertain for the whole of her reign. It was not until the very end of it that Anne proved, decisively and to all the world, that, although a Tory, she was not a Jacobite, and did not wish to be succeeded by the Pretender. For these reasons, divisions between Whigs and Tories, obscured in the 1690s, grew deeper again in Anne's reign.

The reign was dominated by two great statesmen who had served William and were themselves not party men, Marlborough and Godolphin. Apart from winning the war against France, their object, right from the beginning, was to balance Whigs and Tories, as William had tried to do, and to resist both Whig and Tory attempts to capture the ministry for one party. Unfortunately,

Anne seemed less convinced of the virtue of this balancing act than William had been. The balance swung first to one side and then to the other. It swung first to the Whigs, who gradually replaced Tories as ministers until, from 1708 to 1710, the ministry, still under Marlborough and Godolphin, was wholly Whig. The Tory triumph followed, and was greater, for Godolphin and Marlborough themselves were dismissed: Godolphin in 1710 and Marlborough at the end of 1711. Edward Harley, made Earl of Oxford in 1711, emerged victorious. The rest of the Whigs were dismissed, the Whig war policy was abandoned, and Oxford opened the negotiations which led to the Treaty of Utrecht.

Of the younger generation of politicians, who had been children at the time of the Revolution and entered politics just at the turn of the century, three commoners stand out: Walpole, Henry St John (later Viscount Bolingbroke) and James Stanhope. All three were born in the 1670s and first sat in parliament in 1701. This new generation were to be fiercer party men than some of their elders, though the issues which divided them do not always seem very clearly connected with old Whig–Tory principles. The war, for example, and its continuance: what was 'Tory' about wanting to end it in 1708, or 'Whig' about wanting to continue it? The Whigs *did* want to, and, in a sense, this is sufficient answer. Yet perhaps it was not quite sufficient, even for them: they felt also the need to restate old Whig principles, which they called, not quite accurately, the principles of 1689. This appropriation of the principles of 1689 by the Whigs was a great party achievement. This is not to say it was unjustified, for the Tories played into their hands in various ways; they did not firmly contradict the view that the Glorious Revolution was a Whig Revolution, and so began to look half-hearted about Revolution principles; they encouraged Anne to appear as High Church and, by association, a believer in divine-right monarchy; they believed she valued her hereditary title to the throne more highly than her parliamentary title; they seemed lukewarm about the Protestant Hanoverian succession – some even thought that Anne would prefer to be succeeded by the Pretender; and those who did not go as far as this seemed anxious to make the Hanoverians, if they did come, weaker kings than Anne and William had been.

The young Whigs of Anne's reign are particularly interesting because their blend of old principles with new ones set the stage for the politics of the next half-century. They manned the stage after 1714, although they did not man it during Anne's reign. Walpole was one of these young Whigs and, by 1714, a leading and experienced one. He had administrative experience: he was a member of Prince George of Denmark's Admiralty Council (comparable to the later Admiralty Board) from 1705 to 1708, Secretary at War from February 1708 to September 1710 and Treasurer of the Navy from January 1710 to January 1711. All three offices were under the great Marlborough–Godolphin ministry, before and after the Junto group of Whig lords began to enter it and it became predominantly Whig in 1708.

Something of Walpole's outlook can be perceived here. He was a Whig, but, assuming the successful waging of the war to be the great Whig objective, he was willing enough to support the Marlborough–Godolphin ministry whether or not it was mainly Whig in composition. He defended the ministry against Whig attacks, especially attacks on Godolphin's financial policy. His three posts were administrative, and mainly financial in scope, rather than political. They belonged to the group of minor offices which gave their holders a useful insight into the way things were run, and often proved to be stepping-stones to the great offices of state, as parliamentary secretaryships are today. They were not important ministerial offices; but nevertheless Walpole held them in time of war. He therefore gained a knowledge of war administration and foreign affairs which was to be very useful to him later. More important, he gained a knowledge of war finance which was of fundamental importance to him during the post-war period which had to deal with the aftermath of war taxation and borrowings.

As Secretary at War, too, he acted as deputy for Marlborough when he was away on campaign, and came into contact not only with him and with Godolphin, but with the Queen. Walpole's conduct in office established his reputation as a competent and efficient man of business and, above all, as a skilful financier, a man who understood the new kind of public finance which had developed after 1689. He was seen to be clear-headed, shrewd and methodical. He was ready to work hard, quick to see relevant points and, at the same time, equable, lively and good-tempered.

These are useful qualities for an administrator. Walpole's activities in the House of Commons showed that he was a powerful political figure, as well as an efficient junior minister. It would be absurd to say that he was positively helped by the instability of Anne's reign (the comings and goings of ministers, frequent general elections, party quarrels, Church quarrels, quarrels between Lords and Commons), but nevertheless, he gained a varied experience, crowded into a comparatively short time, of office, opposition, the problems of ministers, and the working of the House of Commons. He seems to have been a fairly prominent figure in the Commons right from the beginning, in spite of the story that his first speech was hesitating and awkward. It is not known what this first speech was about. Walpole's first recorded activity in parliament was his successful promotion of a bill enabling his constituency, King's Lynn, to build a workhouse for the poor. This was in April 1701, two months after his election. Perhaps it is an apocryphal story: ugly ducklings turn into more romantic swans than do cygnets.

Walpole's early speeches are described by contemporaries as

'eloquent', 'full of vivacity'. He spoke sensibly and pithily, on local questions at once, and on national questions soon afterwards. In January 1702 he supported the Abjuration Act (which declared the Pretender guilty of treason), and early in Anne's reign he defended William III, spoke in favour of toleration to dissenters, and proposed a Whig Speaker. He was quick to take up legal and constitutional points, and clearly was interested in them. One of these was the famous Aylesbury controversy, a dispute about the powers of the House of Commons in election matters. In July 1702 the mayor of Aylesbury, as returning officer, refused to allow certain electors to vote in the parliamentary election. They applied for redress not to the Commons but to the common law courts, arguing, correctly, that their right to vote depended on the common law. For this the Commons condemned and imprisoned them. The House of Lords supported the electors, so the quarrel was between the two Houses as well as between the Commons and the common law courts. It was a dispute about the qualifications of electors, not about who was elected. The Commons already had jurisdiction in cases of disputed elections; now, in January 1704, the Commons passed a resolution extending its jurisdiction to cover qualifications of electors. Walpole made a spirited attack on this extension: 'Where you say, that the sole Judging of the Qualifications of the Electors, belongs to the House of Commons only, those, I apprehend, are Words of too large Extent and ill Consequence.' His ally was William Cavendish, later (1707) second Duke of Devonshire, who remained a close political friend until his death in 1729. But they were unsuccessful. Their minority view was however shared by some of the best lawyers of the day and, in the next century, came to be generally accepted both by the Commons and by the courts.

Walpole's part in the impeachment of Henry Sacheverell, a constitutional argument of another kind, is a sign not so much of interest as of his prominence in Whig counsels in 1710. The early eighteenth century saw a surge of impeachments. They were, in general, rather clumsy attempts to use a judicial weapon for a political purpose: to get rid of ministers. The 'crimes and misdemeanors' of which impeached ministers were accused were often not illegal at all; for instance John, Baron Somers, chief architect of the Revolution settlement and greatest of William III's ministers, was charged with giving advice to William III about foreign policy. The impeachment of Sacheverell also had a political purpose, though a different one. He was a High Church parson who had preached two sermons in which he supported the doctrines of divine right and passive obedience; he refused to admit that subjects had, in any circumstances, the right to resist their rulers and, somewhat absurdly, denied that the Revolution was based on the right of resistance. He also maintained that the Church was in danger from the degree of toleration afforded to Protestant dissenters.

Sacheverell's sermons were condemned in both Houses, and it was decided to impeach him instead of, for example, leaving the courts to try him for seditious libel. Impeachment was the only sphere in which the House of Lords acted not as a court of appeal, but as a court of first instance, trying an impeached man on charges drawn up and defended by the Commons. The Commons appointed managers to formulate the charges. They were then considered by the House as a whole and, after approval or amendment, the managers presented them to the Lords and argued the Commons' case. Walpole was one of the managers, and also wrote a pamphlet against Sacheverell, *Four letters to a Friend in North Britain*.

Sacheverell was found guilty. He was forbidden to preach for three years, and his two sermons were ordered to be burnt. It is a favourite view of historians that minority opinions in the past might have withered away if contemporaries had been wise enough to ignore them. In this case, some contemporaries also thought that, however wrong-headed Sacheverell's doctrines were, it was impolitic to give him what Chandler, compiler and publisher of Commons debates, described as 'a long and solemn trial, in Westminster Hall, before the House of Lords, an Honour that so contemptible a Tool very ill deserved'. Not all the ministers were in favour of the impeachment: Godolphin wanted it, but Somers thought it unwise. It seems that Walpole agreed with Somers. Certainly, Sacheverell and his supporters knew how to inflame public feeling, There were alehouse meetings, processions, bonfires, rioting. Dissenters' chapels were pulled down. The London mob grew as excited on Sacheverell's behalf as it had been against the Papists, thirty years earlier. By good fortune, the excitement was checked before it could develop into the sort of terror that gripped London in the Gordon Riots of 1780. The lightness of Sacheverell's punishment was celebrated as a Tory triumph. 'I think', Walpole wrote, 'they had as good as acquitted him.'

Nevertheless, the trial proved to be of great value to later generations of Whigs. Its value lay in the statement, in speech and in writing, of the Whig view of the theory underlying the Glorious Revolution. The result was to tie the Revolution and its doctrines, once and for all, to the Whigs. So in 1791 Edmund Burke, seeking definitions of true Whig doctrine to differentiate it from the theories of the 'new Whigs', sympathetic to the French Revolution, found such definitions in the speeches of Walpole and other Whigs at Sacheverell's trial. He wrote:

It rarely happens to a party to have the opportunity of a clear, authentick, recorded declaration of their political tenets upon the subject of a great constitutional event like that of the Revolution. The Whigs had that opportunity.... In this proceeding [the impeachment], the Whig principles, as applied to the Revolution and Settlement, are to be found, or they are to be found nowhere.

Walpole's speech was direct and uncompromising. It was, he said, rubbish to argue that the Revolution was not based on resistance. To deny the right of resistance was 'a matchless indiscretion'; its opposite, the doctrine of 'unlimited, unconditional, passive obedience' was 'first invented to support arbitrary and despotic power'. Nevertheless, the right of resistance could not be provided for in law; it was the people's safeguard just because it was their last resort, to be used when all legal measures had failed.

Resistance . . . is what is not, cannot, nor ought ever to be described, or affirmed in any positive law, to be excusable. When, and upon what never to be expected occasions, it may be exercised, no man can foresee; and ought never to be thought of but when an utter subversion of the realm threaten the whole frame of a constitution and no redress can otherwise be hoped for.

It is this speech that Burke praised, contrasting its clear common sense with the extravagant views of the 'new Whigs', who, he believed, thought of resistance not as a last resort but as an everyday occurrence. Perhaps he was a little unfair to them.

Nevertheless, it is important to note that Walpole's first real contribution to theory was a defence of the Revolution. The whole of the proceedings were printed and published immediately after the trial, enabling us, as Speaker Onslow said, 'to rejoice that this memorial of the rights of the People is always to remain in the records of Parliament'.

The Whigs who had brought the impeachment, however, did not gain from it. Rather, they were blamed for what Daniel Defoe called:

the distracting and turbulent time for the last two months of this year [February and March 1710], occasioned by the Prosecution and Defence of a High-Flying Clergyman, who has undertaken in the teeth of a very Parliament, as well as of the Nation, to justifie and defend the exploded Doctrine of Non-Resistance.

The trial was followed by the period of four years of Tory rule which ended Anne's reign. In these years of fierce Whig opposition, Walpole showed himself clearly as an important political figure in his own right. Although remaining appreciative of Marlborough and Godolphin, he was now a real Whig; he had his own small group of political friends, mostly from Norfolk, and they all supported the Whig Junto lords.

Walpole was now indeed important enough to be a Tory victim. Godolphin was suddenly dismissed in August 1710 and Marlborough, who refused to resign, was disgraced in January 1711. Harley became Earl of Oxford and Lord Treasurer in May 1711. Walpole was dismissed from his post as Secretary at War in September 1710 and, in January 1711, when Harley realized he had no further need of his support, Walpole was dismissed from his post as Treasurer of the Navy. In January 1712, Walpole was accused of corruption, expelled from the House of Commons, and sent to the Tower. It was, as he wrote to his sister Dorothy, 'a barbarous injustice being only the effect of party malice'. He became a Whig hero, indeed a Whig martyr, and perhaps a less moderate Whig than before. In the Tower he was visited, it was said, by all the leading Whig lords, and even had a poem – *The Jewel in the Tower* – written about him; he turned his hand to writing pamphlets and showed that he could write as convincingly as he spoke.

After Walpole's expulsion from the Commons, his constituents re-elected him. The House of Commons, however, resolved that he was 'incapable of being elected again to this present Parliament'; to which resolution he submitted, thus bowing to the House of Commons instead of, as the radical John Wilkes said when expelled from the House in 1768, to the people of England. Walpole's constituents refused to hold another election and the seat remained vacant for the rest of the session.

When parliament was prorogued in July (it was dissolved in August), Walpole was released. During the following autumn, before parliament met again, Walpole published his persuasive pamphlet entitled *A Short History of Parliament*, a fair rejoinder to the Tory apologia, Swift's *Defence of the Allies*. He was elected to the next parliament – the last parliament of Anne's reign – which sat from February to July 1714.

Inevitably, with the Queen's health failing, this parliament was dominated by the question of the succession; it was a question which harassed and divided the Tories, but united the Whigs. Almost at once there was an attempt to expel Sir Richard Steele, journalist and Whig pamphleteer, who had published pamphlets attacking the ministry and accusing it of endangering the Protestant succession. Walpole defended Steele in a 'long and eloquent speech', justifying his charges and attacking the ministry's policy. It was one of the outstanding speeches of Walpole's career.

'This violent Prosecution', said Walpole, was a threat to the liberties of subjects and of members of parliament. Steele had committed

> no other Crime, than his exposing their [the ministers'] notorious Mismanagements; and like a good Patriot, warning his Countrymen against the imminent Dangers, with which the Nation in general, and, in particular, her Majesty's Sacred Person, were threatened, by the visible Encouragement that was given to the Pretender's Friends.

How, Walpole asked, could writing for the Hanoverian succession be 'a reflection upon this ministry'? The defence failed and Steele was expelled by 245 votes to 152. This large majority was, however, greatly reduced when the succession was discussed directly.

In April, during the great debates on the state of the nation and the question whether the Protestant succession was 'in danger under Her Majesty's Government', Walpole spoke forcefully and 'with a great deal of vivacity', arguing that the Queen's name should be removed from the question, for the danger to the succession was not from the Queen, but from the 'dubious Conduct of some Persons'. (It was known by now that not only had Oxford and Bolingbroke approached the Pretender, but also that the Pretender refused to change his religion.)

Walpole was supported by the Speaker, Thomas Hanmer, and a group of thirty or so other Tories. This was a great moral victory for the Whigs, though they lost the question. Tory unity in support of Bolingbroke's Schism Act, to penalize dissenters' schools and academies, was no compensation for disunity elsewhere. Walpole played a prominent part here too, denying that the dissenters were a danger either to Church or to State. But Oxford and Bolingbroke were in power and the parliament was a new one. Its prorogation at the beginning of July, in order to hide the Tory divisions, could not help the Whigs, however united, or put them in power. Only the Queen could do that.

In normal circumstances, the Queen would not have done so. But her illness, soon to prove fatal, combined with Bolingbroke's unbridled ambition, made the circumstances abnormal. Anne's very real concern for her Church and for the Protestant succession, her fear that neither would be safe in Bolingbroke's hands, turned her back to those moderate Whig peers who were a guarantee of the Hanoverian succession.

Hanoverian Whig 1714–21

The Tory triumph of the last four years of Anne's reign, already weakened by the rivalry between Oxford and Bolingbroke – the old and the new generation – was finally wrecked by an approach to the Pretender, apparently with the idea of making him Anne's successor. The original expectation, of course, was that the Pretender would become an Anglican. Oxford, at first successful in keeping the Queen's favour, lost it and was dismissed at the end of 1714. Bolingbroke missed his chance and Anne appointed the moderate Whig Shrewsbury as Lord Treasurer. Two days later, on 1 August, Anne died.

The Protestant succession was now safe. The Regency took over the government. Bolingbroke, who either did not believe or was not deterred by the Pretender's statement that he would not change his religion, was dismissed at the end of August. In September, George I arrived in England, having on his way appointed Townshend Secretary of State in place of Bolingbroke. Marlborough was restored to favour and to his position as Commander-in-Chief. Fearing impeachment, Bolingbroke fled to France in April 1715. In June, Walpole announced the impeachment. In July, Bolingbroke joined the Pretender and became his Secretary of State. Oxford, Ormonde and Strafford were impeached at the same time; Ormonde, like Bolingbroke, joined the Pretender. Oxford stayed, faced a long trial, and was, in the end, acquitted.

In the same year, the Jacobite rebellion gave what proved to be the final blow to the Tory party. Not many Tories were involved, but even this handful of sympathizers was sufficient to tar the whole party. In 1716, Bolingbroke left the Pretender's service and began to think of a return to the English political scene. He became convinced – quite rightly – that the Tory party must have the stain of Jacobitism removed from it, otherwise there would be no hope of its regaining political power. Unfortunately his own conduct – treason in 1714, flight in 1715 – made him an unsuitable instrument for purging or purifying the party. So the Tories, whose fathers sensibly co-operated with the Whigs to turn James II off the throne, allowed themselves to be ruined by being associated with the claims of his Pretender son. George I was therefore tied to the new generation of Whigs in a way in which William III had not been tied to the old. Although George managed to include one Hanoverian Tory, the Earl of Nottingham, amongst his ministers, the arrangement only lasted until 1716. Nottingham then resigned.

Walpole's stature at the end of Anne's reign was high. He was not only one of the leading Whigs in the House of Commons, but also one of the most important in the party. He had suffered for his Whiggism. He had a reputation for administrative competence and financial acumen. He was, moveover, the political associate and brother-in-law of Townshend, the only minister George I appointed before he reached England. Walpole was therefore bound to hold office under the new King. He was appointed Paymaster of the Forces in October 1714, and, a year later, First Lord of the Treasury.

For Walpole, the first seven years of George I's reign were not years of continuous office-holding any more than Anne's reign had been. The first Whig triumph under George I was, indeed, a sort of echo of the Tory triumph after 1710, though it had a happier ending. The first two years were years of settlement: four Tory ministers were impeached, the Jacobite rebellion was suppressed and the rebel lords were impeached for treason. In all these proceedings, Walpole took the lead in the Commons. Then, in the summer of 1716, the Whigs split into two camps, one led by Sunderland and Stanhope, the other by Townshend and Walpole. The split weakened the Whig government at home at a moment of great success abroad. This very success was the immediate reason for the split. Other factors contributed: George I's long absence in Hanover from July 1716 to the end of January 1717; friction between Stanhope and Townshend, the two Secretaries of State responsible for foreign affairs; the influence of George I's German advisers, especially Bernstorff, the Hanoverian Minister of State, who came to England with George in 1714; and bad feeling between George I and his heir, the Prince of Wales.

George I went to Hanover in July 1716, taking with him Stanhope and Bernstorff. It was there that Stanhope negotiated an alliance with France – a diplomatic revolution, taking England away from her war-time allies into an alliance with her war-time enemy. There can be no doubt of the usefulness of the alliance to England. In spite of the defeat of France in the War of the Spanish Succession, she was probably the strongest power in Europe, and certainly the power most likely to help the Jacobites, or at least threaten to help them. The treaty with France provided security against this danger. George I, who was, as Elector of Hanover, engaged in the Northern War, gave his full agreement and encouragement and indeed was anxious that the alliance with France should be made as quickly as possible.

Agreement in England was less certain. France seemed, to most Englishmen, a natural enemy. Moreover, the concept of the balance of power threw doubt on the wisdom of an Anglo–French alliance. It was only two years since the end of a long European struggle to defeat her, and bitter Whig attacks on the Tory Peace of Utrecht, which recognized Louis XIV's grandson as King of Spain, had not been forgotten. Townshend and Walpole, in London, grumbled at the rapidity of the change of allies, wished the King would leave Hanover, and feared that he would involve England in a war with Sweden. They believed, rightly, that Stanhope did not take account of the difficulties of men 'on the spot' in London, poised uncomfortably between an absent King and an ambitious Prince of Wales, and expecting to have to justify in parliament a policy they had not made and about which they had grave doubts.

Stanhope, for his part, thought Townshend and Walpole unsympathetic towards his difficulties and too ready to assume that the interests of the Elector of Hanover must be incompatible with those of the King of England.

It is not surprising that Stanhope's views were congenial to George I. The hope that, once George was back in London, he might come to understand Townshend and Walpole better, was soon dispelled. Bernstorff told the King that, according to his information from London, these two were hobnobbing with the Prince of Wales. As if this were not bad enough, Sunderland journeyed to Hanover specially to tell the King that Walpole and Townshend were deliberately holding up Stanhope's policy. As a result, when George I returned in January, Townshend was demoted from Secretary of State to Lord Lieutenant of Ireland. In April, he resigned. Walpole resigned, too, and a number of others followed, including Pulteney, Methuen and Orford. The ministry was reconstructed around Stanhope and Sunderland.

For the next three years, Walpole was not only out of office, but in open opposition. It was a more perplexing opposition than in the years before 1714, for it was opposition not to a Tory, but to a Whig government. It was also sadder. It is impossible not to sympathize with Walpole's indignation that this real blow to his career had come from intrigues which his old Whig friend Stanhope had either fostered or, at best, taken advantage of.

Your private letter to me [Walpole wrote to Stanhope in December 1716, while he was still in Hanover] I have not let one mortal see. I never read it, but some parts of it astonish me so much that I know not what to say or think. What could prevail on you to enter into such a scheme as this, and appear to be chief actor in it, and undertake to carry it through in all events, without which it could not have been undertaken, is unaccountable.... Think a little coolly, and consider how possible it is for men in a passion to do things, which they may heartily wish undone. I write this as an old acquaintance, that still desires to live in as much friendship, as you will make it possible or practicable for me. And let me once more beg of you to recollect yourself, and lay aside that passion, which seems so predominant in all your actions. I have heard old friends were to be valued like old gold. I never wished anything more sincerely than to bear that title, and to preserve it with you.

Walpole was not deceived by Stanhope's protestations that George I had an implacable objection to Townshend, but not to Walpole. He did not hesitate, though remaining loyal to Townshend might well have meant the end of his career.

The three years of opposition were further complicated by a quarrel between George I and his son. Prince George Augustus had been made Duke of Cornwall in Anne's reign. He came to England with his father in 1714 and was at once created Prince of Wales. He was then thirty-one years old, seven years younger than Walpole. Father and son had not been on good terms in Hanover, and a reconciliation just before Queen Anne's death in 1714 did not go deep or last long. George I's visit to Hanover in 1716 did not help matters. It gave the Prince a taste for power and an additional grievance because his father allowed him only restricted authority. Soon after the King's return there was a public quarrel, and the quarrel was translated into political terms. In December 1717 the Prince was banished from St James's and, early the following year, set up an independent court at Leicester House.

This was the first of the series of quarrels between Hanoverian Kings and their heirs which were to be a factor in politics over the next century. Although these quarrels seemed to be a divisive factor, it may be that, in the first half of the century, they were also a useful one, taming some malcontents into becoming patriotic friends of the Prince of Wales instead of unpatriotic friends of the Pretender. This first quarrel had an unusual and unexpected effect. George I had simple tastes and no love of ceremony. His son, helped by his wife Caroline, had shown himself to be sociable and approachable. During the first two years of his reign, George I had been content that the Prince and Princess of Wales should take the lead in court life and do the entertaining that he found so irksome. In the summer of 1717, George I suddenly changed his habits. A few months after his return from Hanover, and soon after Walpole and Townshend resigned, the King shed his unsociability and became the centre of a generous and hospitable court, all the more attractive because it was not stiff and formal.

George I's new way of life was a shrewd reaction both to the split in the Whig ranks and to his quarrel with his son; and of course it continued after the Prince set up his court at Leicester House. For the next three years, the King's court was a lively and friendly place, and the King mixed with those who came to it instead of retiring to his own rooms. His court was therefore neither deserted nor dull as his son had hoped it would be. Perhaps the King's conduct also helped his ministers. Walpole and Townshend had to go to Leicester House or abjure courts altogether. This they could not do without openly renouncing any hope of returning to office. They were welcomed at Leicester House and continued to visit it until the double reconciliation of 1720, when they returned to office and George I and his son patched up their quarrel.

The offices Walpole held in the two and a half years before he resigned reflected his aptitude and his reputation. They were just right for him. He worked hard and with zest and obvious satisfaction. He was Paymaster of the Forces for a year and then, in October 1715, was appointed to the two offices of First Lord of the Treasury and Chancellor of the Exchequer. The Paymastership was an honourable and a profitable office. Its holder was a senior rather than a junior minister. It gave Walpole a London house – Orford House in Chelsea, next to the Hospital. He kept this house for the rest of his political life and took his title from it when he resigned and accepted a peerage in 1742. It was there that he began to indulge his taste for gardening and for collecting pictures.

Walpole's appointment as First Lord of the Treasury in 1715 was promotion to one of the great offices of state. He turned at once to what was generally regarded as the most frightening of the post-war problems: the vast and unprecedented size of the national debt and the high rate of interest payable on it. He held office just long enough to come to certain conclusions and to make proposals. His successors as First Lord, Stanhope until 1718 and then Sunderland, implemented only a part of his comprehensive plan. Their own contribution to solving the problem was their acceptance of the South Sea Company's offer to take over a large part of the national debt. This proved disastrous and led to the crisis which was Walpole's immediate problem when he returned to the Treasury, succeeding Sunderland, in 1721.

The great old financial officer of state was the Lord Treasurer. Lord Treasurers were peers, or were created peers on appointment, and sat in the House of Lords. Occasionally in the early seventeenth century, and often after 1660, the office of Lord Treasurer was put in commission – that is, the Lord Treasurer's duties were given to a board of commissioners, usually five. The reason for this administrative device was political, to avoid concentrating so much power in one man. The Treasury was in commission for the whole of William III's reign. In Anne's reign, however, it was only put in commission once, and only for six months, from August 1710 to March 1711. Godolphin was Lord Treasurer from 1702 to 1710, Oxford from 1711 to 1714 and Shrewsbury in 1714.

George I at once reverted to William III's practice and none of his successors departed from it, so that there has been no Lord Treasurer since 1714. The Treasury Board consisted of the First Lord and usually four others, including always the Chancellor of the Exchequer, who was also Under-Treasurer. Until 1827, it met regularly to transact business but, in the eighteenth century, there was a growing tendency for its members, other than the First Lord, to be not front-rank politicians but juniors, often at the beginning of their career. This eighteenth-century development, which put the First Lord in a position not very different from the old Lord Treasurers, unencumbered by a Board, hardly affected Walpole's position in 1716. It was, however, affected by his simultaneous appointment as Chancellor of the Exchequer.

The appointment of one man to the two offices of First Lord of the Treasury and Chancellor of the Exchequer was a novelty. The Chancellor was the most important of the junior members of the Board. He might be called the 'Second Lord'. He had judicial functions, as well as being Under-Treasurer. Nevertheless he was a subordinate financial minister, not of cabinet rank. The combination of his office with that of First Lord increased the First Lord's power in relation to the rest of the Board. The two posts had only once before been held by the same man – this was Charles Montagu, who became Chancellor in 1694 and kept the office when he was appointed First Lord in 1697. He resigned both in 1699. Although Walpole's combination of the two posts lasted only for eighteen months in 1715–17, he combined them again, for twenty-one years, from 1721 to 1742. The precedent was followed by all later First Lords who were commoners until 1834 when Peel, though in the Commons, appointed a separate Chancellor. The Chancellor of the Exchequer then became an important office-holder in his own right.

It was, however, not financial power, even at the beginning, that made the vital difference between Walpole's position and the position of the Lord Treasurers. It was status. Walpole was not a peer. This equally distinguishes his position from that of earlier First Lords. Only three commoners had held office as First Lord of the Treasury before Walpole: Laurence Hyde in Charles II's reign; and Sir James Lowther and Montagu in William III's reign. None of the three held office for more than two years, and all three became peers soon after they left office. Walpole's tenure of office was short, too. The real significance of having the government's financial head in the Commons instead of in the Lords, thus linking the Commons' control of finance with the minister responsible for financial policy, was seen after 1721, when Walpole held the offices of First Lord and Chancellor of the Exchequer for twenty-one years without leaving the House of Commons.

This link between the Treasury and the House of Commons, forged just about the time new financial techniques were being worked out, had a vital and permanent effect on English political life. It was, in a sense, an unbroken link for, if the First Lord was a peer, the Chancellor of the Exchequer was in the Commons. No other minister had a link of this kind with the Commons. It strengthened the eighteenth-century House of Commons just as certainly as did the main legislative achievement of 1716, the Septennial Act. The first Act to prescribe a maximum duration of parliament was the Triennial Act of 1694, which prescribed one of three years. Few of the parliaments between 1694 and 1716 lived out their maximum life. There were ten general elections during these twenty-two years, a breathless and chaotic period, which certainly proved that a maximum of three years was too short.

The Septennial Act raised the maximum to seven years. More important, there was also born the idea that parliament's legal maximum life should also be its normal life, that every parliament had a right to live for seven years. Practice matched theory: during the next twenty-two years, to 1738, there were only three general elections. There were eight general elections in the first fifteen years of Walpole's parliamentary career (to 1716); in the twenty-five years from 1716 to his resignation in 1742 there were only four. The contrast is striking. It is the more striking if one remembers that it was not simply the result of a statute: there was nothing after 1716 to prevent general elections from being as frequent as before it. Nevertheless, there began at once a series and a habit of regular and long parliaments, lasting, on average, six and a half years instead of two and a quarter.

This was one of the principal differences between political life before and after Walpole's first tenure of high office, and one of the fundamental facts about Hanoverian parliamentary government. There had never been long, regular parliaments before. This perhaps does not give Walpole his due. The Bill began in the House of Lords and was introduced by Devonshire, one of Walpole's oldest political friends, who was with him in the Commons until 1707. There is no evidence that Walpole was its originator, but he was its constant champion and defender. He was, however, ill and unable to be in the House of Commons when the Bill was discussed there, so what he would have said about it in 1716 must be guessed from his arguments against the proposal to repeal it in 1734.

Walpole's zeal for the Septennial Act is matched by his zeal against the Peerage Bill of 1719, the chief legislative project of Stanhope and Sunderland, who displaced him in 1717. This was based on an entirely novel principle: the House of Lords was to be changed from a body whose size depended simply on the number of peers that the King created, into a body with a fixed maximum size. Clearly, there is some sort of connection between these two important constitutional measures, the Septennial Act and the Peerage Bill, each of them, in the eyes of their supporters, settling and strengthening one House of Parliament. The connection is difficult to define, for both of them did more than this. Both affected also the relationship between the three partners in parliament – King, Lords and Commons. This is the main reason not only for widely differing views about both measures, but also for different views about the connection between them.

Walpole believed that support of the Septennial Act went with opposition to the Peerage Bill. Stanhope and Sunderland believed that opponents of the Septennial Act would support the Peerage Bill. They even hoped that an offer to repeal the Septennial Act would persuade the Commons to like the Peerage Bill. This strange offer was never made, mainly because the Lord Chamberlain, the Duke of Newcastle, wisely insisted that it was misconceived. Walpole was more correct in his diagnosis than Stanhope and Sunderland. Eighty-eight members of the House of Commons who had voted for the Septennial Act voted against the Peerage Bill. Only ten who had voted against the Septennial Act voted for the Peerage Bill. One hundred and twenty-seven voted against both.

The Peerage Bill was introduced into the House of Lords in March 1719. It provided that the House of Lords, which then had 220 members, should, in future, be restricted to a maximum of 235 members. The number of English peers was not to exceed 184, six more than the existing number; the anomalous sixteen Scottish elective peers, introduced by the Act of Union, were to be replaced by twenty-five hereditary ones; the number of bishops was to remain at twenty-six. These proposals at once became the subject of fierce debate in the press. The main argument for the Bill was the 'abuse of the prerogative', in 1712, by Queen Anne, who created a dozen Tory peers 'all on one day' in order to increase support, in a predominantly Whig House of Lords, for the Tory peace policy. One of the charges against Oxford at his impeachment was that he had advised this creation, 'being most wickedly determined, at one fatal blow, so far as in him lay, to destroy the freedom and independency of the House of Lords'. It was thought essential, to preserve the balance of the constitution, that there should be no more blows of this kind.

The main argument against the Bill also looked to the balance of the constitution. It asserted that the Peerage Bill would make the House of Lords so strong, so independent of both King and Commons, that the balance of the constitution would be destroyed.

It was outrageous to force the King to surrender his prerogative for this purpose. These arguments won a respite. Because of what Stanhope called 'strange apprehensions' in the country and the likelihood of 'great opposition in the other House', the Bill was withdrawn before the third reading in the Lords. But it was not dropped. It was introduced again at the beginning of the next session in December. The King sent a message saying that he had the 'settlement of the peerage' much at heart and did not wish his prerogative to stand in the way. The Bill passed the Lords, but was defeated in the Commons – on the motion to commit – by 269 to 177 votes.

This defeat was one of the great victories of Walpole's career. He had already taken part in the pamphlet controversy. In the Commons, he was the Bill's chief opponent, with Steele, also a pamphleteer, as a vigorous second. Walpole spoke, said Speaker Onslow, 'with as much of natural eloquence and of genius as had been heard by any of the audience within these walls'. His speech was also elegant. It began with a passage admirably suited to introduce a defence of a constitution often termed 'classical'. For to Walpole's contemporaries 'classical' had reference to the constitution of Ancient Rome and its likeness to the mixed or balanced constitution of eighteenth-century England.

> Among the Romans, the wisest People upon Earth, the Temple of Fame was plac'd behind the Temple of Virtue, to denote that there was no coming to the former, without going through the other: But if this Bill pass'd into a Law, one of the most powerful Incentives to Virtue would be taken away, since there would be no coming to Honour, but through the Winding-Sheet of an old decrepit Lord, and the Grave of an extinct noble Family.

Few people have ever regretted the defeat of the Peerage Bill. This is mainly because the things it would have prevented did not happen, or at least did not happen for a long time.

Anne's abuse of the prerogative of creating peers was not repeated and, until 1783, the House of Lords remained as small as it would have had to be if the Bill had passed. Yet the battle itself was not much ado about nothing. Immediately, of course, the defeat proved that governments could not do without House of Commons support, and that they would be more comfortable with the leading member of the Commons in the government and not in opposition to it. This was not a new lesson. A newer lesson was suggested by the fact that the Commons had prevented the Lords from reforming itself. This is the greatest surprise of this surprising battle. All the members of the government were peers, and the two parts of parliament directly affected by the Bill, King and Lords, were both in favour of it. Yet the wishes of the House of Commons prevailed and the Bill was dropped. This suggested that, whatever the balance between King, Lords and Commons meant, it did not mean legislative equality.

This was Walpole's most important argument, even if it was implied rather than stated. His arguments are particularly interesting because they state his views on the nature of the constitution ten years or so before he began to be accused of modifying it. He defined the constitution as a balance, an equilibrium of King, Lords, and Commons. This is orthodox enough. What is significant is his definition of balance. It was, he said, a balance of dependent powers, not of independent powers. The Peerage Bill would turn the House of Lords into a closed, oligarchic body, independent of its two partners.

> For as there is a due balance between the three branches of the legislature, it will destroy that balance, and consequently subvert the whole constitution, by causing one of the three powers, which are now dependent on each other, to preponderate in the scale. . . . The lords will now be made independent of both [the other powers].

He condemned the Bill for taking away the royal prerogative of creating peers, so making it impossible for the King to reward 'virtue and merit'. He asked whether 'the abuse of any prerogative is sufficient reason for annihilating that prerogative?'. He argued that the Septennial Act had not increased the power of the Commons in the way that the Peerage Bill would increase the power of the Lords, for the Septennial Act had not taken away the King's prerogative of dissolving parliament. Finally, Walpole asked:

> What is the abuse, against which this bill so vehemently inveighs, and which it is intended to correct? The abuse of the prerogative in creating an occasional number of peers, is a prejudice only to the lords, it can rarely be a prejudice to the commons, but must generally be exercised in their favour.

This, perhaps, is the vital argument. The King's prerogative of creating as many peers as he wishes is useful to the Commons. It may weaken the Lords; even its abuse will strengthen the Commons. This is not far from asserting the primacy of the Commons, as, in practice, Walpole was asserting it by securing the defeat and dropping of the Bill.

The Commons defeat of the Peerage Bill was a personal triumph for Walpole. It was also a step, though not a very large one, towards office. It gave Stanhope and Sunderland another proof of the government's weakness in the Commons, and Walpole's ascendancy there, and it made them drop the Peerage Bill. But they had the King's support and there was no question of Walpole's replacing them. At most, he might be asked to rejoin them, and this would mean having Townshend back too. There were disadvantages as well as advantages in such an arrangement. During the next few months, however, the latter came to outweigh the former. One cause of this was the discovery that Bernstorff, who in October 1719 had been forbidden to interfere in English affairs, was for that very reason intriguing to replace Stanhope and Sunderland with Walpole and Townshend.

This was Bernstorff's last fling in England. It probably disposed Stanhope and Sunderland to think that, with Walpole in office, they would at least be safe from plots of this kind. It also disposed them, and others, to try to patch up the quarrel between the King and the Prince of Wales. This was done in April 1720. The Duchess of Kendal helped. Walpole persuaded the Prince to submit, not very gracefully, to his father. In the Commons, Walpole supported Stanhope's proposal to pay the King's civil list debts. The general reconciliation included, in June 1720, a return to office for both Walpole and Townshend. Neither, of course, returned to the office he had left. Walpole returned not to the Treasury, but to his old office of Paymaster; Townshend became not Secretary of State but Lord President of the Council. And there they might have stayed if the South Sea Bubble had not burst in the autumn of 1720.

3
POLICY
1721–42

FOR MOST PRIME MINISTERS, policy is a measuring rod for achievement. Their achievement is large or small in proportion to their success in putting their policy into effect. Walpole's policy and achievement are not related in this way. His policy provides a measuring rod for his performance in office, but it does not provide one for his achievement. This is because his achievement was on a level which, for most Prime Ministers, is already firm and fixed when they take office: the basic structure of political life and its working relationships. Walpole was also largely responsible for the lasting settlement of the Hanoverian dynasty, but this, although an important achievement, is not a fundamental one.

Because Walpole's achievement *is* fundamental, and because it is not obviously connected with his policy, it is easy to overlook his policy altogether, or to underestimate it. Yet the very fact that Walpole had a policy at all is one of the remarkable things about him. This policy, both domestic and foreign, shaped England in the 1720s and 1730s. It was Walpole's policy, not the King's. How remarkable this was can be seen by looking back only two generations. In William III's reign, the initiative in policy lay with the King; in Anne's reign, it lay with those who could command her favour; in the 1720s and 1730s, it lay with Walpole. The success of Walpole's policy of course helped the settlement of the Hanoverian dynasty, but this was not the mainspring of his policy. In foreign affairs, inevitably, the dynasty was more obtrusive than in domestic affairs. It would have been undesirable at any time to outrage kings of England by ignoring the interests of the other country they ruled. It was impossible to do so in the 1720s and 1730s, when the maintenance of the Protestant succession, which meant the Hanoverian dynasty, was the main concern of British foreign policy. In domestic affairs, however, Walpole was freer. He had a policy and objectives quite independent of the dynasty. He would have tried to implement this policy in any circumstances and under any dynasty. His policy can be seen more fairly if, for the moment, his achievement is put on one side. Peel, one of 'the great practical politicians' who praised Walpole, took off his constitutional spectacles to do so. It is useful to follow Peel's example. He wrote, in 1833, to Philip Stanhope, great-great-grandson of the Stanhope who ousted Walpole in 1717:

> Of what public man can it be said with any assurance of certainty, that, placed in the situation of Walpole, he would in the course of an administration of twenty years have committed so few errors, and would have left at the close of it the House of Hanover in equal security, and the finances in equal order? – that he would have secured to England more of the blessings of peace, or would have defeated the machinations of internal enemies with less of vindictive severity or fewer encroachments on the liberty of the subject?

First Lord in George I's reign 1721–7

Walpole rejoined the ministry in June 1720 as a subordinate. Neither Stanhope, nor Sunderland, nor the King intended Walpole to be a leading member of the government. His financial skill might suggest his suitability for the posts he had left in 1717, but it seemed unlikely that he would regain them. Stanhope, who had replaced him as First Lord of the Treasury and Chancellor of the Exchequer in 1717, became Secretary of State again in 1718. The two Treasury posts were then separated: Sunderland became First Lord and John Aislabie became Chancellor of the Exchequer.

Walpole's return to the Treasury less than a year later was therefore unforeseen and unintended. It was not a straightforward promotion, as in 1715, but the result of the need to reconstruct the ministry after the havoc caused in it by the bursting of the South Sea Bubble. The Bubble was pricked in August 1720 and the ensuing collapse lasted over the next two months. By December, when parliament met, the extent of the disaster was clear and, as it happened, the worst of the crisis was over. The need was to still the panic, clear up the company's affairs, and learn the lesson. This was, for the government, caution: to be sceptical of schemes which promised to pay off the national debt painlessly, even profitably, and not to be dazzled by the magical properties of the stock market. Naturally enough, public opinion was more concerned with the immediate past than with the future; there was a deep desire for vengeance on the directors of the company who had conceived the scheme which led to the Bubble and on the ministers who had accepted that scheme. This desire was felt and expressed both inside and outside parliament. By March, the ministry had suffered two resignations and two deaths. It was the resignations which created the vacancies that Walpole filled.

Aislabie, Chancellor of the Exchequer, who was found guilty of corruption and expelled from the Commons, resigned in January 1721. Sunderland, First Lord of the Treasury, though cleared of the charges against him, resigned in March. Walpole was appointed to both posts. Stanhope died in February, after a stroke which followed his fiery defence of the ministry in the House of Lords, and was succeeded by Townshend. The other Secretary of State, James Craggs, died in March, on the same day as his father, who was Postmaster General. Craggs was succeeded as Secretary of State by Carteret, friend and follower of Sunderland. Sunderland remained in the ministry as Groom of the Stole, one of the most important court offices, to which George I had appointed him in 1719. He retained the King's favour and it seems clear that he was still considered the leading member of the ministry. Indeed, in this period after Stanhope's death, Sunderland was sometimes called a Prime Minister, a clear sign that this label did not go with any particular office.

For his part, Sunderland bided his time. He was not content, but he knew that the reconstructed ministry need not last. Walpole and Townshend had achieved important ministerial positions again, but this was only an accidental achievement and could sooner or later be righted. Walpole was, for the time being, an unfortunate necessity; Townshend was balanced by Carteret, and might be dislodged as he had been in 1717. Indeed, they might both be dislodged. A general election was coming and might help things along. All this changed overnight in April 1722, when Sunderland suddenly died.

His death made Walpole and Townshend the most important members of the ministry. Walpole was, however, not more important than Townshend. In fact, they seemed to be repeating the Stanhope–Sunderland position before 1717, when Stanhope was still in the Commons. Stanhope and Sunderland had sometimes been called 'the Prime Ministers'; their relative power was a question that was never resolved. The same question, applied to Walpole and Townshend, was resolved when Walpole assumed an overlordship of foreign affairs, in addition to the responsibilities of his own office. This did not begin to happen until the mid-1720s.

There was no thought of overlordship in 1722. But Townshend had nevertheless great need of Walpole's help and Walpole was very ready to give it. Townshend needed help because he disliked and distrusted Carteret, the other Secretary of State; and Walpole, too, thought Carteret a potential source of mischief and danger. Carteret was now the chief representative of Sunderland's former followers, and was regarded as a great expert on German affairs. George I liked him and found him sympathetic to Hanoverian problems. No doubt he told the King, as Stanhope had done, that English and Hanoverian interests had much in common. Walpole knew as well as Townshend did that this was an argument unlikely to be palatable to either House of Parliament.

Their concern illustrates one of the greatest difficulties that beset the conductors of English foreign policy in the eighteenth century. There was no foreign minister. Responsibility for what is now the Foreign Office lay with two Secretaries of State, whose duties were divided geographically and therefore, of course, frequently overlapped. Carteret and Townshend both went to Hanover with George I in 1723, so that at least Townshend was not in London when Carteret planned a repetition of the 1716 intrigue, this time finding an ally in Bernstorff, who saw the intrigue as a way of recovering some of his lost influence in English affairs. They failed. George I was more aware of what was happening than he had been in 1716, partly because this time Townshend also had an ally on the spot, the Duchess of Kendal, who, for the rest of George I's reign, was to prove an invaluable and honest intermediary between the King and his ministers.

In April 1724 Carteret was dismissed from the secretaryship and sent to Ireland as Lord Lieutenant. He was succeeded as Secretary by Newcastle, once a Sunderland man but now firmly for Walpole. These changes, and the support of the Duchess of Kendal, made for a homogeneous ministry and greatly strengthened Townshend's and Walpole's positions. They were also strengthened, in 1724, by the appointment of Walpole's brother Horatio as ambassador to France.

This was, in the eighteenth century, the most important British embassy. Horatio Walpole was a career diplomat, a great contrast to the noblemen who often held the post, and was hard-working, cautious and resourceful. His knowledge was much respected and he had the happy knack of not making personal enemies. He was of great service to the government, not only for his work in Paris, but for his activities in the House of Commons. He was frequently called from Paris, especially at the beginning of a session, to explain the government's foreign policy, and he was often to be found discussing it with individual members. His speeches were full of information, facts, dates and figures. Even more important, he generalized from these and explained the overall objectives of policy.

His activities in the House of Commons were the more valuable because both Secretaries of State, Townshend and Newcastle, were in the House of Lords. Townshend, unfortunately, did not get on with Newcastle, whom he found over-cautious. In the crisis of 1725–6, however, Townshend seemed not only obstinate, but also bellicose and liable to panic. The crisis arose because the two powers most dissatisfied with the Treaty of Utrecht, Spain and the Empire, composed their differences and made an alliance, the first Treaty of Vienna. It was Townshend's reaction to this that led Walpole to his first interference with foreign policy.

To Townshend, the Treaty of Vienna was a step towards the creation of a vast empire, uniting the Habsburg lands and Spain, 'more formidable to the rest of Europe than ever Charles vth was, by reason of his [the King of Spain's] relation to the crown of France'; it also opened the door to a Jacobite invasion supported by Spain and the Emperor. As a security against these dangers,

Townshend negotiated a counter-alliance, a defensive alliance between England, France and Prussia. Though the Treaty was again negotiated in Hanover, the dangers it guarded against were dangers to England and not to Hanover. Walpole's interference in 1725 was not with policy, but with its presentation. The dangers, he thought, were not as imminent as Townshend believed. There was no immediate danger of a Jacobite invasion, and it must not be suggested that there was any such danger. The policy must be put to parliament not aggressively, but calmly and moderately. This was done in the Commons by Horatio Walpole. There was little criticism, and the Treaty of Hanover was endorsed by large majorities in both Houses. The voting in the Commons was 285 to 107 and in the Lords 98 to 25.

Four years later, Walpole interfered more decisively. Townshend was in Hanover at the time, and Walpole took negotiations between France, England and Spain out of his hands, giving them to the Council at home on the grounds that they 'being on the spot [were] better judges of the present temper and disposition of the nation'. The resulting Treaty of Seville broke the Spanish–Imperial Alliance. It halted the commercial rivalry between Spain and England and also, more ominously, ended the estrangement between France and Spain.

A quarrel between Walpole and Townshend followed and, in May 1730, Townshend resigned. He was succeeded by William Stanhope, who was created Lord Harrington. Walpole now had final authority for, and oversight of, foreign affairs. It was not only Townshend's temperament that made such oversight badly needed – it was also the lack of unity inevitable in the division between two Secretaries of State. Townshend apparently believed that, having got rid of Carteret, he could also get rid of Newcastle; and this forced Walpole to choose between Townshend and Newcastle. It is not surprising that, in the end, he chose Newcastle. They had many views in common and no serious difference until 1737. They both regretted Townshend's bellicose anti-Austrian policy and believed that the restoration of close relations between France and Spain meant that England should move towards Austria, though this of course carried the risk of cool relations with France.

Home affairs, however, were Walpole's main concern in the first years after his appointment in March 1721, and indeed for most of the remainder of George I's reign; and, in particular, financial and economic affairs in which he had won his reputation. First was the problem of the South Sea Company and the greater problem which underlay the scheme which had led to the disaster: the national debt.

In William III's reign, the government debt became the debt 'of the nation', in the main guaranteed by parliament and secured by parliamentary funds. This made the debt safer, and unlikely to be repudiated. In Anne's reign, especially under Godolphin, the techniques of long-term borrowing were developed, but the idea of a permanent debt was not accepted: the general view was that the debt should be small and that the ideal was government with no debt at all. This general view was not shared by Walpole. He did, however, believe that the debt should be prudently managed: this meant some repayment, some rearrangement and some reduction of interest. In 1716, during his first short period at the head of the Treasury, Walpole devised a comprehensive plan for dealing with the 'Debts of the Nation' – the title of the pamphlet he wrote in 1712. Stanhope adopted part of the plan when he succeeded Walpole in April 1717, and this part was embodied in an Act of Parliament. The Act provided for the reduction of interest on most redeemable government debts from six to five per cent, simplified the revenue by grouping it into a number of funds, and established a sinking fund to be fed from three funds and to be applied to reducing the debt. The problem of high interest rates on irredeemable annuities, which Walpole had intended to deal with, was not touched. This problem underlay the South Sea Company's scheme.

This was one reason why, in the autumn of 1719, the government was disposed to welcome the South Sea Company's proposals to take over this part of the national debt and offer government creditors South Sea stock in exchange for their holdings. Another reason was the apparent success of the similar scheme in France, devised by the Scottish financier John Law; this, it was said, would soon entirely wipe out the French government's debts. Aislabie, Chancellor of the Exchequer, was particularly attracted. Walpole was not in office when the Company's scheme was adopted; he criticized it in the House of Commons and, in March 1720, tried unsuccessfully to include in it a definite statement of the value of South Sea stock in terms of government annuities to be exchanged for it. The absence of such a statement certainly encouraged the directors to push up the price of stock, and the public to speculate. Speculation was wild, widespread, and quite uncontrollable. The Company's capital was artificial and hopes of real profit were imaginary. The Bubble was bound to burst. It burst in August, and the simultaneous collapse of markets in France made things worse in both countries.

Walpole was then Paymaster. This does not mean that he took no part in suggesting measures to meet the crisis. He took a leading part, although there was obviously less authority behind his suggestions than there was to be after March, when he was again made First Lord of the Treasury. 'The wonderful Mr W—le', as the *London Journal* called him, was indeed expected to produce a plan to restore credit, and of course he was helped by the fact that he had criticized the scheme before it was accepted. In December, he produced a plan for 'ingrafting' South Sea stock into the Bank of England and the East India Company; it was accepted, but the ingrafting was made voluntary and not very much was done. Even more important were Walpole's efforts, before and after he became First Lord in March, to prevent a witch-hunting regime of punishments and impeachments. This meant persuading the House of Commons not to agree with the view expressed by the leading country Tory, William Shippen, whose demand in December for the punishment of all concerned in the acceptance of the scheme was repeated in April:

by this time a whole Nation call'd aloud for Vengeance; and if they neglected to hear the Voice of the People, it would look as if they had a Mind to provoke them to do themselves Justice . . . the only effectual Means to restore Credit, was to call those to a strict Account, who had ruin'd it.

Walpole's efforts had some success. The directors were punished but, on the whole, less vindictively because of Walpole's intervention. The only member of the government to be punished for his part in the affair was Aislabie, who was certainly guilty. It is likely enough that, but for Walpole, Sunderland would not have been acquitted. Walpole's moderation, however, did not make him popular. Indeed, it won him a nickname that was to cling to him all his life – 'Skreen Master General'. (The 'Skreen', hiding and protecting corruption, inspired popular prints in 1721 and reappeared in 1742.) But it was of great benefit to the country that this, the sharpest financial crisis of the century, was also comparatively short and did not leave a legacy of political and social unrest.

The Company's future was settled in August 1721; its trading capital was reduced and, by 1750, it was no longer a trading company. The Bank of England came to its rescue – the crisis had strengthened the Bank's position, making firmer the links between it and the government. Walpole's handling of the crisis added greatly to his prestige. Moreover, as Walpole said, although the scheme was faulty and its management disastrous, the structure of the national debt was certainly improved by the exchange of a large volume of government annuities for South Sea stock. The crisis and the scandal left other legacies too: a great horror of the 'infamous practice of stock jobbing', and a great concern for probity and integrity in public life and in the conduct of public finance. The second legacy was of very great value.

The sinking fund, set up in 1717, caught the public imagination, as did Walpole, who was acclaimed as 'father of the sinking fund' although he had left office before it was established. It was generally regarded as the most important part of the 1717 reform, simply because most people were more concerned with reducing the national debt than with managing it efficiently and cheaply. The security represented by the sinking fund perhaps played its part in the conversion of public opinion from the old view that a national debt meant that the country was on the verge of bankruptcy to the new view that a national debt meant national credit, so that a large debt was a sound and useful investment and a sign of confidence in the country's stability and well-being.

This new view, with its corollary that wiping out the debt should not be the first object of government policy, took time to establish itself; there were hints of it in the generation or so after the war, but usually they were fiercely contradicted. To most of Walpole's contemporaries the sinking fund was valuable simply because it held out the possibility that the debt would be progressively reduced and, at some future date, extinguished. Therefore the management of the sinking fund tended to be judged, in any one year, by the amount of debt reduction. By this criterion, it was successful in George I's reign but less successful in George II's. This was because, in George II's reign, Walpole came to use the sinking fund not only to reduce the debt, but also to cover potential deficits in current income. Some of these deficits were the result of reduction in taxation, for example a lower land tax. Walpole was therefore using the sinking fund as an alternative to increasing, or anyhow not reducing, taxation. This was much censured by his opponents, who asserted, quite wrongly, that the debt was not being reduced at all. It was also censured, later, by the younger Pitt, who fell into the absurd trap of continuing to feed his new sinking fund, even when he had to borrow at high rates of interest in order to do so.

Walpole's defence is convincing. He explained, in 1735, that the sinking fund had grown much larger than had been estimated in 1717, partly as a result of a further reduction of interest on most of the national debt, in 1727–30, from five to four per cent.

> The Sinking Fund has now grown to a great Maturity, and produced annually about 1200000 l, and was become almost a Terror to all the individual Proprietors of the Publick Debts ... the great monied Companies, and all their Proprietors, apprehend nothing more than being oblig'd to receive their Principal too fast; and it became almost the universal consent of Mankind, that a Million a year was as much as the Creditors of the Publick could bear to receive, in discharge of part of their Principal.

It is obvious today, when borrowing and tax yields go together to make up a government's revenue, that a national debt policy and a taxation policy are two sides of the same coin. It was less obvious in Walpole's time. However, it is clear that what Walpole achieved was a position in which taxation, together with the hereditary revenue, more or less covered expenditure; and absence of war enabled this position to be maintained. The amount of new, long-term borrowing during Walpole's time at the Treasury was therefore very small. Moreover, the lowering of the war-time level of taxation enabled him to treat taxation not only as a way of raising revenue, but also as part of an overall plan for the economy. It was not easy to do this in the 1720s and 1730s, when the popular view – that Englishmen were over-taxed – was reinforced by the view that taxation added to a government's power as well as to its revenue, by creating a horde of prying and tyrannical tax collectors, as bad – if not worse – than a standing army.

Walpole's taxation policy was based on a preference for indirect over direct taxation. The main direct taxes were a window tax, assessed on the number of windows in the house, and a land tax. Walpole disliked the land tax, which had originally been intended to apply to other forms of property as well. Its exclusive application to land could hardly be reversed, but nonetheless he thought it unwise. The tax had other drawbacks: it was unequally assessed and the money collected was not remitted promptly to the Exchequer. Walpole wished to reduce it from its war-time level of four shillings in the pound and hoped, ultimately, to abolish it altogether. He kept it down to two shillings in the pound for nearly every year from 1722 to 1738, and reduced it to one shilling in 1732 and 1733. He believed that indirect taxes on consumable goods, handed on to the consumer and paid for by a small and widely distributed increase in price, could be fair, productive and not burdensome. There were problems, however, about the existing indirect taxes. The chief ones were customs and excise duties. Walpole defined the difference between them: customs duties were a tax on the import of commodities; excise duties were a tax on their consumption. Excise duties were efficiently collected – this was partly because excise was a comparatively new tax, only dating from 1643, and partly because evasion was difficult. Customs duties, the oldest indirect tax, presented a very different picture. They were complicated, unwieldy to collect, and easy to evade. The Book of Rates had not been brought up to date. Some articles attracted duty at several different rates, introduced at different times. Smuggling was a widespread and lucrative occupation. Walpole tackled all these abuses. He revised the Book of Rates, increased the penalties on smuggling, and reduced some prohibitive duties in order to make smuggling less profitable. These were sensible and workmanlike administrative measures; they did not, however, stop the loss through smuggling.

Walpole therefore introduced a plan for taxing imports in a new way, not at the ports but at a later stage. It was a new plan, not simply a tightening up of existing methods, and it had advantages quite apart from the raising of revenue. The plan was introduced in 1723, and passed as an Act of Parliament. It provided that certain articles should be imported free of customs duty and stored in government warehouses until needed, either to be sold to customers or to be re-exported. If they were sold, duty would be charged and collected by excise officers; if they were re-exported, no duty would be charged. The articles to which this system of bonded warehouses was applied were tea, coffee and chocolate. The duty they paid, if not re-exported, was not technically a customs duty but an internal duty, a duty on consumption. This was in effect, though not in name, a transfer from a customs duty to an excise duty. The plan was successful: that is, it increased revenue and decreased smuggling. It had another object, not financial but commercial. The system of bonded warehouses facilitated and so encouraged the growing colonial re-export trade. London was pushed nearer to the position that Walpole wanted for it as the centre of a thriving re-export trade, 'the free port of the world'.

Indirect taxation in general, Walpole saw, served purposes other than the raising of revenue. Tariffs were bound to affect foreign trade and internal economic development, and could be made to encourage them along particular lines. In 1721, an Act was passed abolishing nearly all customs duties on the export of British manufactures and on some raw materials. This Act completed the process of reducing export duties which had been going on slowly since the 1690s. It won great praise. George Chalmers, author of the valuable *Comparative Strength of Great Britain*, first published in 1782, wrote that the year 1722, when the Act came into force, 'must always form an epoch, as memorable for a great operation in commercial policy as the establishment of the sinking fund had been in finance a few years before'. Import duties on raw materials used in manufacture were reduced; and some duties on the import of raw materials which England could not produce herself – silk for example – were abolished. This policy led later economists and politicians, and historians too, to see Walpole as the father of the industrial revolution. Some – Gladstone for one – saw him also as taking the first step on the road to free trade. It might perhaps be called the 'protective step'. Taxes on imported manufactures were not abolished, and some were increased, for example by the Calico Act passed 'to preserve the woollen and silk manufactures and for more effectively employing the poor'

First Lord in George II's reign 1727–42

Not even the Jacobites stirred when George Augustus, Prince of Wales, succeeded his father in June 1727. This was undoubted evidence of the growing stability of the dynasty, and owed something to Walpole's policy during the past six years. Nevertheless, the immediate question for Walpole was the new King's attitude to him and to the other ministers. All offices were automatically vacated by the death of a King, a sign that ministers had by no means escaped from being the King's personal servants, who might or might not be continued in their offices when a new king succeeded to the throne. George II's opinion of his father's ministers could hardly be unaffected by his opinion of events since 1720. This was low. His reconciliation with his father in 1720 had, of course, been superficial; the fact that it went hand in hand with the reconciliation of the two Whig camps had rendered Leicester House innocuous, and this George found humiliating. In particular, Walpole had deserted Leicester House. Because of this and other desertions, George II could have no hope in 1727 of making a ministry out of his Leicester House friends. Nevertheless, he felt impelled to make some gesture to prove his difference from his father. The gesture he made was to tell Walpole 'to take his orders from the Speaker' [Spencer Compton]. It was an odd phrase. It is not easy to know what George really meant, and perhaps he did not know himself.

Of course everyone thought, either fearfully or hopefully, that it was the first step to Walpole's dismissal. But the second step did not follow. For a month, everyone waited for the arrangements that must be made if Spencer Compton were to be, as Newcastle put it, 'the chief man' of the new reign. Walpole and Compton worked together in preparation for the meeting of parliament at the end of June. Of course, Compton could not compare with Walpole in ability, but this fact does not explain the outcome of this short, sharp crisis. Spencer Compton was a good Speaker; he had no great political capacity or following, but what he did have was the King's liking. Perhaps George knew – or was persuaded – that this was not enough. Certainly Queen Caroline, ambitious for power herself, was convinced that Walpole must stay and did her best to convince the King. Probably George was always more set on showing that he *could* dismiss Walpole rather than on actually doing it. At any rate, on 24 July Walpole and the other ministers were confirmed in their offices. Caroline regarded this as a victory for herself and so, in part, it was. But by the end of the year, if not before, George II's loyalty to Walpole no longer depended on the Queen – it was his own; deep and, in his own words, 'for life'. So Walpole entered on the second stage of his ministry, with no rivals among his colleagues and no equals except Townshend, no

Hanoverian favourites to contend with, and royal support more certain and more unreserved than under George I.

Yet, with all these advantages won, Walpole's policy is less clear-cut and less easy to pinpoint in George II's reign than in his father's. One reason is that foreign affairs came to be more and more dominant; and, as Walpole himself said, foreign policy depended on responses to situations not in his control. Another reason perhaps is that there were no spectacular inventions in either financial or economic policy, as there had been earlier, although there were modifications of past policy, and extensions of it. These, however, were attacked by the opposition as innovations, a left-handed tribute to his earlier policy. Indeed, possibly the main reason why Walpole's policy is less easy to discern after 1727 is that it met with more conspicuous opposition – conspicuous in that his opponents now included a number of discontented Whigs. This strange opposition, and his dealings with it, obscure his policy as it was not obscured earlier. Tories, Jacobite Tories and disgruntled Whigs were not easy bedfellows, and the addition of the Prince of Wales's party did not make them easier. Nevertheless the opposition groups were, in the 1730s, sometimes persuaded to co-operate. Their co-operation did not produce a united opposition, but it produced an articulate and often a vociferous one. They attacked Walpole's policy, but often less vehemently than they attacked his responsibility for it. In this way, Townshend's resignation in 1730 is a landmark because it left Walpole with undisguised final authority in foreign, as well as in home affairs. He became a 'Prime Minister', open to attack as the holder of an unconstitutional position.

In the 1730s, attacks on policy are so interwoven with attacks on Walpole as 'prime' or 'sole minister', and on Walpole's system, that it is difficult to disentangle them, let alone be fair to either kind of attack. Attacks on the system took a well-worn path, and from this one may deduce that the system itself was neither as new nor as peculiar to Walpole as the attackers maintained. There were Pension Bills, Place Bills, complaints that parliaments lasted too long, and attempts to reduce the size of the already tiny standing army. These were traditional ways of trying to reduce the so-called king's influence; they can all be found during Charles II's long parliament (1661–79), known as the 'Cavalier Parliament'. These attacks on the system are all in a way reactionary, or nostalgic, looking back to a golden age when no placemen – holders of office under the crown – sat in parliament, when there was a new parliament every year and when England was defended not by a standing army, but by its militia. It was no doubt a mythical golden age: but the fact that people looked back to it is significant. It explains why, when Walpole was attacked not in the traditional way but in a new way, it was for his innovations. 'Almost every Session', said Pulteney in 1740, 'introduces something new, in diminution of the Liberties, or derogatory to the Constitution of this Kingdom.' The basis for attack was the same: the innovations were suspected of being introduced in order to strengthen the government against the Commons, or against parliament as a whole.

It was this suspicion that prompted complaints against a number of what seemed to be sinister changes in parliamentary procedure. For example, the Address in reply to the King's Speech at the beginning of a session had once simply been a brief expression of thanks and loyalty; but, over the years, King's Speeches had grown longer, and were now well known to be not personal messages from the King, but statements of government policy: to match them, the 'new form' of the Address mentioned every item in the Speech. This, it was said, was deliberately misleading, conveying the false impression that the Commons unanimously approved the entire policy of the government, 'It looks', Pulteney said, 'as if the Parliament had in a Lump approved of all the Measures of the Administration.' The new practice of holding Cockpit meetings of government supporters (in the Tudor Cockpit between Downing Street and Whitehall), on the eve of a new session, to hear the King's Speech read, was deprecated. These were 'Ministerial Conventions . . . *novel Assemblies*', pernicious because they undermined the Commons' independence. Government encroachment on the Commons was blamed for the modern habit of passing the annual Mutiny Act as a matter of course instead of after long discussion and debate, as in the past, and for the new-fangled practice of having Finance Bills drafted by 'Gentlemen of the Treasury'.

Financial policy, as well as procedure, was attacked, and was indeed a constant and popular target. The grounds for attack were the same: innovation and the strengthening of the government. Votes of credit, for example, were attacked because they empowered the government to raise money without asking parliament, 'at best a *temporary Suspension of our Constitution*'; the use of the sinking fund for current income was condemned as unconstitutional, tampering with a 'sacred Fund'; the excise scheme was denounced as tyrannical because it would increase the number of revenue officers.

The excise scheme is, in fact, the most blatant example of Walpole's policy being obscured by the clamour of his opponents. His policy was a financial and commercial one, and he recommended it with financial and commercial arguments. So, also, did later economists: in 1776 the father of political economy, Adam Smith, praised Walpole's 'famous Excise scheme' for its advantages both to trade and to the revenue; in 1838, J. R. McCulloch, economic theorist and public servant, described the scheme that Walpole failed to effect – but which was successfully introduced by Huskisson in the 1820s – as 'one of the greatest improvements ever effected in the commercial and financial policy of the country'. Walpole's opponents, however, attacked the excise scheme with constitutional arguments. They did not meet his arguments at all, and they ignored his replies to theirs. Walpole's intention was to extend the bonded warehouse system, introduced in 1723, and by 1733 a proven success, to two more commodities: tobacco and wines. Because of opposition out of doors, he decided to deal with the two commodities separately, beginning with tobacco. The opposition's determination not to meet him on his own ground was apparent even before he introduced his proposals in the Commons. In February 1733, Walpole gave notice that he would move for a Committee of the Whole House to enquire into the state of the public revenue. He referred to the 'very great Frauds committed in the collecting of the publick Revenue', and believed that a plan to reduce them would be 'of very great Advantage to the publick Revenue and also to every honest and fair Trader'. To this, the Tory Sir William Wyndham disingenuously replied that he did not know what the plan was, 'but by all I could ever yet hear of it, I believe, when it is laid before us, the Question thereon will appear to be, whether we shall sacrifice the Constitution to the preventing of Frauds in the Revenue'.

In March, after this inauspicious beginning, Walpole explained his plan. He spoke simply and clearly, showing its advantages to the revenue and to the re-export trade, and its disadvantages to 'none but Smugglers and unfair traders'. 'I am certain', he said, 'that it will be of great Benefit and Advantage to the publick Revenue, and will tend to make London a free port, and by consequence, the Market of the World.' He even showed that the duty payable on tobacco for home consumption would be reduced from 6⅓d to 4¾d a pound. Although he had supporters, they could make no headway against the rousing but irrelevant arguments of their opponents. Wyndham's rallying cry for the defence of the constitution had more appeal than Philip Yorke's commonsensical question:

> What can the Affair now before us have to do with our Constitution? . . . The only Consideration before us now is, Whether we shall allow those gross Frauds and Abuses, formerly committed in the Tobacco Trade, to be still carry'd on with Impunity, or accept of a Remedy which . . . will considerably improve the publick Revenue, will be of great Advantage to the fair Trader, and of singular Use and Benefit to the whole Nation.

In April, with his majority melting away and opposition unabated out of doors, Walpole decided to abandon his scheme. He produced no more plans which could be labelled 'excise' though, as he said, 'in my private opinion I still think it was a scheme that would have tended very much to the interest of the nation'; but he continued with those financial and economic policies which either needed no fresh parliamentary approval or could be effected by himself alone.

Amongst these were certain administrative reforms, especially in the Treasury itself, and the tightening of the financial link between the Treasury and the House of Commons. A routine parliamentary financial year was established, a timetable for the presentation to the Commons of proposals for expenditure and for the raising of money to meet it, and their discussion afterwards in Committees of Ways and Means and Supply. This was a House of Commons programme, rather than a parliamentary programme, vital for the smooth working of relations between the Commons which controlled finance and the ministers in charge of financial policy. The year began with Walpole's 'opening of the budget', a new phrase popularized by Pulteney in 1733 in a pamphlet portraying Walpole as a quack doctor with his bag of pills and potions.

As if to match the Treasury's increased importance, a new

Treasury was built. The Treasury's rooms in the old Whitehall Palace rebuilt by Wren in the 1680s had been destroyed when most of the Palace was burnt down in the fire of 1698. Since then the Treasury had been housed among the jumble of Tudor and Stuart buildings in the area between Whitehall, Downing Street and St James's Park. This area was known as 'the Cockpit', since the old Tudor Cockpit stood on part of it. In 1732 the Treasury's accommodation at the Cockpit was reported by the Board of Works to be 'in a ruinous and dangerous condition' and 'not safe for your lordships to remain in it'. It was decided to build a new Treasury, also on the Cockpit site. The choice of William Kent as architect brought Palladianism to English government buildings. Here Walpole demonstrated his taste for fine architecture and furnishings, as he was to do on an even grander scale at Houghton Hall.

The new Treasury Chambers were ready for occupation in 1736. They faced north, on a site adjoining the south side of the Horse Guards' Parade, on which in 1753 the new Horse Guards building was to be erected on Kent's plan. Kent's Treasury can be seen today, not from Whitehall (which is fronted by an early nineteenth-century building) but from the Parade. Its north front, which forms an impressive part of the south side of the Parade, is crowned by a great triangular pediment, containing the royal arms and supported by four Ionic columns. The interior of the building contained some splendid examples of Kent's mastery of domestic decoration. After 1736 Cockpit meetings – those Walpolian novelties so disliked by Pulteney – were probably held in the Treasury Board Room, a spacious room on the first floor, about thirty feet square and nearly as high, beautifully proportioned, with an elaborately carved marble chimneypiece and an overmantel of carved wood with a niche for a bust. This room still contains some of its original furniture, notably a magnificent set of twelve upholstered mahogany chairs with cabriole legs, the State Chair used by the King when he presided at board meetings, and a pedestal clock with an astronomical dial made by the famous clock-maker Charles Clay. The massive mahogany table, which matches the twelve chairs, was probably made a little later.

The windows of the Board Room face west, towards the walled garden of 10 Downing Street. Until 1732 No. 10 was a private house, and another house had been built behind it. George II then offered the crown lease to Walpole, who accepted it not for himself but for his office of First Lord of the Treasury, to which post he got it annexed for ever. In this way Walpole established what has ever since been the official residence of the First Lord of the Treasury. The conversion was carried out by Kent and, basically, his alterations created the structure which is now No. 10, the small front house on Downing Street leading into a larger, more formal house behind it, which contains the great staircase, an imposing kitchen, and an official dining-room and drawing-room. The conversion was completed – and its purpose symbolized – by the construction of passages connecting No. 10 with the new Treasury Chambers.

In the early 1730s, Kent also decorated and furnished Walpole's new house at Houghton, built close by the old Walpole family home. The new house was magnificent: sober and dignified, set in fine parkland and gardens planted with a mixture of native and exotic trees and shrubs. It was designed by Colen Campbell, master of the English Palladian house and author of the very influential *Vitruvius Britannicus*, Volume 3 of which, published in 1725, contains the plan of Houghton. Its state rooms were described by the famous engraver and collector George Vertue as 'all finely adorned and furnished with great variety, rich furniture, carving, gilding, marble, and stucco works – every room in a different manner; but the great collection of noble original pictures exceeds all others in numbers and variety'. This was praise of Walpole as well as of Kent, for there is no doubt that Walpole, far from simply hiring Kent to do the work, was himself deeply and continuously involved in the embellishment of his house, as he was with its setting, the park and gardens.

Walpole's youngest son, Horace, visited Houghton in 1736. He was then nineteen, a fastidious Cambridge undergraduate with aesthetic tastes, expecting, it seems, not greatly to enjoy himself. He was surprised to find himself delighted not only with the incomparable pictures, but with the house and with the park and gardens, which he found 'much adapted to my romantic inclination'. He was also delighted with his father. 'As fine as [Houghton] is', he wrote, 'I shou'd not have felt half the satisfaction, if it had not been your doing. I wish all your other Actions cou'd afford you as much ease to enjoy their success, as Those at Houghton.' Indeed, the prim and precious Horace Walpole's admiration for his father – 'the wisest man I have seen' – is a pleasing and convincing tribute to him, if only because it so clearly surprised Horace.

The conduct of foreign policy allows great scope for make-believe and is, therefore, always a useful target for an opposition. It can pretend that the government it opposes is omnipotent, and can talk as if Europe, or the world, is the government's chess board. With Walpole, the constitutional thread which runs through all opposition intensified the make-believe. Walpole's 'sole responsibility for the state of Europe' was taken right back to the Treaty of Hanover, for which he was not responsible and which he had not liked. Being 'a catspaw of France' was laid at his door, as was 'supineness' towards Spain. Yet opposition bellicosity against England's 'natural' enemies, France and Spain, was accompanied by an incongruous demand for a reduction of the standing army from 18,000 to 12,000 men!

The most important factor in the European situation in 1730 was that the alliance with France was loosening. Its value to France, mainly dynastic, had once been great, but was much lessened when the birth of an heir to the throne of France in 1729 removed any uncertainty regarding the succession. France began to follow an independent policy in the Mediterranean and in the Baltic. What was really alarming, however, was the tightening of relations between France and Spain, both now ruled by Bourbons, and the hostility of both to the Austrian Habsburg Emperor Charles VI. This was a revival of the old Bourbon–Habsburg antagonism which seemed, now, only to have been lying dormant since 1715. Walpole wanted to make this situation less dangerous. He wished to keep the French alliance, however feeble it now appeared, but thought it unsafe to have this alliance as the main determinant of English foreign policy. This meant looking towards Austria, the old ally. Walpole had never liked the anti-Austrian slant of Townshend's policy, which he thought provocative and serving no interest except that of France: his rejection of Townshend's plan to help France to build up opposition to the Emperor within Germany, by subsidizing German princes, had been one of the reasons for Townshend's resignation. Townshend's policy was now reversed. Negotiations with the Emperor Charles VI began. They were successful, and the second Treaty of Vienna was signed in March 1731.

The Treaty was a turning point in Anglo-French relations. England guaranteed the 'Pragmatic Sanction' – the law settling the succession to the whole Habsburg inheritance in the Emperor's eldest daughter, Maria Theresa; the Emperor agreed to the Treaty of Seville. But the guarantee of the Pragmatic Sanction was, of course, unacceptable to France: there was even talk of war between England and France. And, in 1733, the family feeling that had been growing between the French and Spanish Bourbons was cemented in the first Family Compact. Unfortunately, English relations with Austria began to cool in the mid-1730s – this was mainly because Walpole regarded peace in itself as a vital English interest. The Emperor maintained that England was bound by her 1731 alliance to help Austria in the War of the Polish Succession. George II was ready for war; but Walpole was determined that England should not support Austria in a war that, as he said, could not be regarded as defensive and had nothing to do with the Pragmatic Sanction. In this he succeeded: England stayed out of the war. The 'good offices' for peace, extended by Walpole to both France and Austria and at one time seeming likely to be taken up, were now rejected. If England had not stayed out of the war, Charles VI would no doubt have turned down the French offer of mediation in 1735 – certainly he would have had warmer feelings towards England. But, even if Walpole could have foreseen the future, he would not have conceded that the Emperor's warm feelings were worth a war to which England was not bound by treaty. This, then, was his reply to his critics in 1741–2; to have kept England out of the War of the Polish Succession was a success, not a failure. His critics denounced it as a failure, saying, quite rightly, that this policy had left England without reliable allies. Both, perhaps, are plausible views.

Walpole could not claim success, and indeed did not try, in the question of the war with Spain. His failure lay not so much in policy as in being unable to raise support, either in parliament or in the country, for a peaceful settlement of the quarrel with Spain. The quarrel was about trade with the New World, a hangover from the Treaty of Utrecht, and, in particular, about the Spanish claim to have the right to search English trading ships. English public opinion was outraged; and Walpole's agreement with Spain, the Convention of El Pardo, in 1739, had little chance of doing more than postpone hostilities. In fact, it did not even do that: Spain did not want postponement any more than English public opinion did. This was not (yet) a European quarrel and had nothing to do with the balance of power, although it was believed that France would, in the event, support Spain. In October 1740, however, the Emperor Charles VI died. The scene shifted and, within a year, the colonial and naval war was swallowed up in a European contest about the Austrian succession. In December of that year, Frederick II of Prussia, soon to be 'the Great', invaded Silesia. France was now the leader of a powerful alliance designed to partition Maria Theresa's territories; England, under the agreement of the Pragmatic Sanction, decided to send help to Maria Theresa. This was a blow that the enfeebled alliance between England and France could hardly stand. Even so, the formal ending of diplomatic relations between the two countries came not then but in 1744 (after Walpole's resignation), when France refused to expel the Young Pretender who was preparing to invade Britain. The refusal was a return to the traditional French policy, held at bay for nearly thirty years, of supporting the Jacobites and thus threatening the English Protestant succession.

4
ACHIEVEMENT

The Settlement of the Hanoverian Dynasty

ENGLAND in the 1730s was a prosperous country. Trade had been increasing steadily since the early 1720s; harvests were good; the level of wages was higher than in the past; and the cost of food and drink was lower. Walpole's economic and financial policy had contributed directly to this happy state of affairs and therefore, indirectly, to the settlement of the Hanoverian dynasty. Prosperity at least showed that the constitution established in 1689, after the Glorious Revolution, and the Protestant succession guaranteed by the Hanoverians, were compatible with, even if they did not cause the general welfare of the country. Two parts of Walpole's policy were more directly concerned with the security of the dynasty or, rather, of the Protestant succession: foreign policy and policy towards the Jacobites. These two parts were not separate. The main danger from the Jacobites was always that the Stuarts might be restored not by an English uprising, but by a foreign army: this is what the Stuarts hoped for. Just as Charles II in exile before 1660 had angled for help from the courts of Europe, especially France and Holland, and James II in exile after 1689 had set up his little court at St Germain, so his son, the Old Pretender, and his grandson, the Young Pretender, dreamed of a French invading army in 1715 and 1745. They dreamed also of help from

Spain, Sweden, Austria, the Pope, even Peter the Great. Perhaps none of the powers which played with the Pretenders would have helped them for their own sake; yet it is clear that not only France but other courts constantly over-estimated the volume of Jacobite support in England. To seem to be willing to help the Pretenders was a useful diplomatic weapon. In particular, it was a traditional French weapon. The French refusal to expel the Pretender in 1744 was proof enough that Walpole had been wise to base foreign policy primarily on a possible Jacobite appeal to foreign courts, especially the French court, and only secondarily on the vague concept of the balance of power.

The link with Hanover had advantages and disadvantages. It gave Britain, a European power, a territorial foothold in Europe. The union with Holland under William III had done this less decisively, partly because Holland was, like England, a sea power, and was on the edge of Europe, while Hanover was in the middle. Holland was a great power, Hanover only a second-rate one. Nevertheless, Hanover had friends and enemies of its own in Europe, not only in Germany, but among the Baltic powers – especially Sweden and Russia. Its enemies might well toy with the Jacobites, to hurt England and Hanover together.

At home, the Jacobite threat was in the main a unifying factor. This was natural, for the Stuarts remained Catholics, and this could not be forgotten even if their love of absolutism was played down by the suggestion that they would, if again restored, hold the crown on the same conditions as the Hanoverians did. Yet this was only half the story, for the outcome of the 1715 rising, and of the Jacobite plots of 1717 and 1720, depended not on wide English support but on foreign help. In the face of this, it can hardly be said that the danger was exaggerated, nor that the danger was small because the number of English Jacobites was small. The final proof of the need for vigilance was the 1745 rising: even this was not doomed to fail should foreign help be forthcoming.

The so-called 'usefulness' of Jacobitism to Walpole is sometimes taken as proof that he deliberately and dishonestly exaggerated a danger that he did not himself fear. Of course it does not prove anything of the kind. Moreover, all the evidence is that he did fear Jacobitism. Nor was the danger itself particularly useful: for example, it took English foreign policy into paths that, but for Jacobitism, few would have wanted. The association of the Tories with Jacobitism was perhaps more useful. Bolingbroke had probably done more than anyone else to fix this association in the public mind, and his recantation in 1716, and hard work afterwards to de-Jacobitize the Tories, could never quite undo the damage. Nor did the Tory leaders in parliament undo it. Certainly Walpole did not help the Tory leaders in the Commons, Wyndham and Shippen, to rid the Tory party of the taint of Jacobitism. Why should he? Shippen indeed paraded his Jacobitism, which perhaps proved that, like other so-called Jacobites, he was willing to drink the Pretender's health but not willing to bring him back. Shippen's failure, and even more Wyndham's failure, to resurrect a party willing and able to play an effective role in politics, cannot be blamed primarily on Walpole. It was at least partly due to the inadequacy and disunity of the Tory leaders that, before the end of George I's reign, Tories who wished to take part in politics were sliding away from calling themselves Tories, and were calling themselves opposition Whigs or some other kind of Whigs.

It can hardly be doubted that this slide to the Whigs was a sign that the Hanoverian dynasty would last. There were two conditions. The Hanoverian Kings must not step outside the limitations imposed in 1689 and 1701, and English policy must not seem to be swayed by Hanoverian interests. Walpole ensured that both these conditions were fulfilled; and the Hanoverians themselves – George I and George II – were not unhelpful. Although they were less able than William III, much less important in European affairs, and completely foreign while he had been half English, they nevertheless had certain advantages which he lacked. They ruled a small German state, not, as he did, a great European power. They did not seek to initiate policy in England. Even in foreign policy, they were on the defensive – their main fear being that Hanover might be sacrificed to English interests. This was of course a real danger, much more likely to happen than the much-feared sacrificing of England to Hanoverian interests. They had sons. George I was the first English king for a long time to die leaving an adult male heir. Moreover this heir had, at the time of his father's death, two sons of his own. This ruled out both the uncertainty of the last two reigns and, in 1727, the possibility of a repetition of 1714. No one doubted that George, Prince of Wales, would succeed his father and become George II.

The presence of an adult male heir throughout George I's reign, and for most of George II's, had another result. Neither King got on with his eldest son. Both sons, from time to time, indulged in politics and provided a focus for political opposition to the King and the King's ministers. Although this set problems for Walpole in both reigns, and contributed to the difficulties which led to his fall in 1742, it may have contributed to the stability of the dynasty, for support of the Prince of Wales against his father was at least a loyal opposition, in the limited but very important sense that it was not anti-Hanoverian.

The Constitution

In the middle of the nineteenth century, people chose to define their constitution as 'parliamentary government', and to give this a special meaning. It would therefore be misleading to apply this description to Walpole's achievement, for this would imply that his practice was the same as mid-nineteenth-century practice. Nevertheless, Walpole set the stage for the particular form of constitution which obtained in England for the next century. He was the first actor on the stage, as well as the first manager. But he saw the problems in terms of the past. To make this kind of claim for one man invites scepticism, but I believe it is justified. After all, others have claimed for themselves a deliberate constitutional purpose. Peel, for example, claimed that his object after 1832 was 'to make the Reform Act work'. Walpole might have claimed that his object was to make the principles of 1689 work. Indeed, he did claim this. Peel did not approve of the Reform Act; Walpole *did* approve of the Glorious Revolution: both saw that the principles they were 'making work' could not work automatically. Perhaps the kind of working relationship that Walpole achieved was implicit in 1689; certainly some people, up to and beyond 1832, thought that it was. Even so, it did not come automatically, and it had not come before Walpole's time at the Treasury. Did Walpole, then, fulfil the principles of 1689, or did he deny them? Did he innovate, in the sense of changing the constitution? This is the basic argument, at the time and ever since. It can be expressed as Walpole versus Bolingbroke. This may seem an odd juxtaposition, an unreal contrast between Walpole's practice and Bolingbroke's theory. This is not so. Walpole was not all practice: there is enough theory in his speeches and pamphlets, and in those of his supporters, to provide a fair contrast in the field of theory. What one lacks is a contrast in the field of practice. Here, Walpole stands alone, and at a disadvantage.

There is no doubt that a great deal of Walpole's practice *was* innovation. He did not follow precedents; he set them. To his supporters, this simply meant that no one before Walpole had found the way to reconcile 1689 and stable government. To his opponents, his innovations implied a theory which was a travesty of 1689: they implied the dependence of parliament, particularly the Commons, on the government. So here at the outset is one reason why Walpole was at a disadvantage: much of the criticism of his practice is really criticism of theory, of the conceptions on which his practice is supposed to be based.

Walpole's fundamental innovation in practice was his own position. To be a Prime Minister, to have more of the King's confidence and therefore to be more important than the other ministers, was not new. It *was* new that a Prime Minister should be a member of the House of Commons and, moreover, neither heir to a peerage nor of a noble family, as many members of parliament were. But the striking novelty was to stay in the House of Commons, and to stay there for twenty years. It is this, more than anything else, that provides the real contrast with the leading politicians of the previous two reigns, and with any man previously called a Prime Minister. And it was a deliberate choice on Walpole's part.

The House of Commons was greatly strengthened by Walpole's presence in it for so long. The Commons, rather than parliament as a whole, became the deciding factor in the continuance or otherwise of a minister's power. Walpole's description of his own position, in 1739, reveals his feeling for the Commons and his pride in his ascendancy there.

> A Seat in this House is equal to any Dignity deriv'd from Posts or Titles, and the Approbation of this House is preferable to all that Power, or even Majesty itself, can bestow: therefore when I speak here as a Minister, I speak as possessing my Powers from his Majesty, but as being answerable to this House for the Exercise of those Powers.

This was no King's man: it was a kind of Prime Minister never known before. Walpole's resignation in 1742, when he had lost the 'approbation' of the Commons but not the favour of the King, completed the story. The whole was a precedent of fundamental importance. It created a model, a standard for future ministers to aim at. None wholly attained it.

Together with this must go the linking, once and for all, of the Treasury with the House of Commons. Walpole's combination of two Treasury offices, First Lord and Chancellor of the Exchequer, and the fact that the other members of the Treasury Board were subordinates rather than near-equals, made him not very different in power from the old Lord Treasurers. This provides visible measure of the change: Lord Treasurers sat in the House of Lords. Walpole's twenty years in the Commons, opening budgets and coping with Committees of Supply and Ways and Means, established a habit of business, a time-table which still remains the basis of Commons financial routine.

It is impossible to exaggerate the importance of Walpole's social background or, rather, his lack of social standing compared with his rivals and – later – colleagues. The eighteenth century is usually thought of as being aristocratic, whereas in fact many members of the aristocracy were simply commoners who had been promoted – and one would have expected Walpole to have been one of them. Walpole was a middling country gentleman 'of no great Family, and of but a mean Fortune' when he entered politics, as Wyndham said in 1734. His family was a provincial family, important in Norfolk but, even there, only one amongst other Norfolk families, and with no court or even London connections. He is not like anyone else, unless it is John Pym, another provincial country gentleman and great Commons leader. This again points the contrast. Pym's ascendancy in the Commons led him to opposition; Walpole's led him to being the King's minister and, indeed, Prime Minister. Walpole's contemporaries looked for a parallel to William Cecil, later Lord Burghley, who managed the House of

Commons for Queen Elizabeth. A print of 1740, for once favourable to Walpole, compared him to Burghley, the 'Patriot-Statesman'. Cecil, also, was not of noble family; but his family was not a provincial one, like Walpole's. His father held a post at court and Cecil rose to power through his services to the Queen, and was directed by her to manage the Commons. This was a very different rise to power from Walpole's.

Of course, Walpole owed his appointment as First Lord of the Treasury to the monarch in much more than the technical sense in which Peel or Russell did in the 1840s. Of course, too, he was never *appointed* as Prime Minister, nor asked to choose his colleagues. These are obvious and basic differences between Walpole's position and that of later Prime Ministers. Walpole and the other ministers cannot be called 'the executive'; they must be called 'the King's ministers'. Their relation to parliament cannot be called 'parliamentary government', if by this is meant a state of affairs where the 'executive power and the power of legislation are virtually united in the same hands'. Ministers were not changed as a body. They were chosen and changed by the King, in ones and twos: they were not chosen at the same time as a general election, and because of its result, as they are today.

After 1867, the period of the so-called two-party system set in, which seemed, to Gladstone and Disraeli, the natural state of British politics. It presupposed two parties, each with a leader and potential Prime Minister, with one of the parties, as the result of a general election, producing a government and having a majority in the House of Commons, and the other party being in opposition. Walpole had an opposition throughout the ten years or so that he was called 'Prime Minister', but it was not a tangible opposition like this. There were two sides, but their composition varied. There was neither a recognized leader of the opposition nor an alternative Prime Minister. The opposition fluctuated in size and in content. It was composed of groups and individuals who opposed sometimes but not always; even the Tories did not always oppose. This fluidity made accurate calculation of support and opposition impossible; and this was a source of strength for the House of Commons as a whole, as against any set of ministers.

Walpole's achievement of a fairly stable support for the government, over a long period, is of immense importance. It did not strengthen the government as much as it strengthened the Commons. It showed that the support of a majority of the Commons was the most vital factor in a government's strength and survival, and it showed, too, that the best way to get this support was for the King to have as Prime Minister the most prominent and able man in the Commons, even if all the other ministers were in the Lords. In this sense, it introduced a new relationship and a new era.

This new relationship did not upset the balance of the constitution, or that of the legislative trio – King, Lords and Commons. But it did emphasize the interdependence of the three. It repudiated the idea that the three parts should be either independent or equal, and also the idea that the King, as head of the executive, should not be mixed in the legislature as well as having part in the passing of bills. The emphasis on interdependence is a legitimate interpretation of the principles of 1689. King, Lords and Commons are partners in legislation; there is no reason why they should not be partners in government too, the King choosing his ministers, most of the ministers sitting in the Lords, but the Commons being the vital factor in the support of the government. This is balance, and this is what Walpole achieved.

5

TWO CRISES AND TWO SIDES

THE ATTACKS on Walpole in the 1730s were, in part, like the attacks on any man in power, simply attempts to get him out and replace him by the attackers. For some of the attackers, they were more than this, as they are in a different way for us. For one thing, they show how important competence was and how difficult it was to get rid of a really competent minister. They show the increasing puzzlement and frustration which were caused by the spectacle of a minister in power for longer than ever before, not only in living memory, but in the known past. They show the dawning of the horrid fear that Walpole might go on for ever, and the understandable deduction that this unnatural length must be the result of sinister practices. This deduction was of course quite illogical and, a generation or so earlier, impeachment might well have been the answer; yet no one thought it possible to get rid of Walpole in this way. Even right at the end, in 1741, the case put against Walpole was not that he was guilty of crimes or misdemeanours, but that 'common fame' justified a demand from both Houses that the King dismiss him.

Some of Walpole's opponents differed from him on policy. Carteret, for example, disagreed with him on foreign policy, and Sir John Barnard, merchant and, in 1737, Lord Mayor of London, on financial policy. But most of Walpole's opponents attacked not his policy, but his position and the 'system' which seemed to them to support it. In concrete terms, the system meant, first and foremost, placemen and long parliaments. The first was not new, but the second was. The combination seemed to give Walpole unprecedented power. These attacks demonstrate what some, perhaps many, contemporaries thought about Walpole's achievement, and certainly show that they did not understand it. Walpole was accused of being a Prime Minister, as Oxford had been, but he was also accused of introducing 'innovations', new practices, to increase his power. Attacks of this kind emphasize that the stability Walpole achieved was a constitutional stability and not a political one, and that it was precarious, to say the least. This is why his long tenure of office, which angered his opponents so much, was so very important. Twenty years was long enough to establish habits of mind and working which, luckily, could not be undone: understanding and appreciation only came later. In fact Walpole was, for his contemporaries, a Prime Minister and something more. This 'something more' was the novelty which his opponents could neither understand nor accept. Walpole was the most prominent man in the House of Commons and in him, for the first time, prominence in the Commons was joined not with leading the Commons against the King, but with being the King's most important minister. A Prime Minister in the ordinary sense was bad enough, but this was worse. It was a double perversion.

It was for this that Walpole's opponents attacked him in the crises of 1733–4 and 1741–2.

Before 1730, Walpole's troubles had little to do with conceptions of government. Nor did his troubles come from parliament, where the Tory opposition was negligible by 1725. They came from rival ministers and, to some extent, from the King and from his Hanoverian friends and advisers. These were the traditional troubles of ministers.

In the second half of the 1720s, these troubles seemed largely overcome. The deaths of Stanhope in 1721 and Sunderland in 1722 seemed to complete the healing of the breach amongst Whigs which had put Walpole and Townshend out of office in 1717. But the two ministers left from the Stanhope–Sunderland group – Carteret and Henry Boyle, Lord Carleton – were not easy colleagues. Carteret was generally thought brilliant, but unsteady. He had never sat in the Commons and had no real following. His intrigue against Townshend failed and, in 1724, he was removed from his post as Secretary of State and sent to Ireland as Lord Lieutenant. Newcastle replaced him as Secretary of State. At the same time, Newcastle's brother, Henry Pelham, a member of the Treasury Board since 1721, was appointed Secretary at War. Philip Yorke became Attorney General. In the next year, Carleton was replaced as Lord President of the Council by the Duke of Devonshire, who had held this office from 1714 to 1717 and left it when Walpole resigned. Sir Peter King was made Lord Chancellor and created Baron King.

George II's accession in 1727 was the only occasion in Walpole's career after 1721 when there was a real danger that the monarch might turn against him. When this danger passed, and Walpole and all his colleagues were confirmed in office, George II announced his intention of keeping Walpole as long as they both should live; it was soon apparent that, as far as royal support went, Walpole's position in the new reign was stronger than before; both he and the Protestant succession seemed to be settled and secured at the same time. Three years later, Townshend's resignation increased Walpole's power and enhanced his position in relation to his colleagues. This at least partly explains why 1730 was also the beginning of serious attacks on Walpole's position and on his system.

The First Crisis 1733–4

It was during the last two sessions of George II's first parliament that opposition to Walpole flared into a crisis. These sessions saw, for the first time, an attack on his policy and also an attack on what was called his 'system'. Both targets were popular, and gave the opposition much support in the country. The policy attacked was the Excise Bill of 1733; the system was attacked by a Place Bill and by a proposal to repeal the Septennial Act. This was the first attempt to repeal the Septennial Act, unless one counts the extraordinary plan of Stanhope and Sunderland in 1719. Place Bills, however, had been introduced long before Walpole's time. The first was in 1675 and the most extreme in 1701, in the Act of Settlement. There were several in Anne's reign. The wonder is perhaps that there had been none before this in Walpole's time at the Treasury. These were the sixth and seventh sessions of the parliament which had met in 1727. It was dissolved in April 1734 and there followed the third 'septennial' election.

The 'famous Excise scheme', as Adam Smith called it forty years later, was an important part of Walpole's financial policy. It would more accurately be called the bonded warehouse scheme, or system. But this is a dull, unemotive label, and it was called the excise scheme from the start. It was a second application of the policy invented ten years earlier. It had then been applied, without opposition, to tea, coffee and chocolate; and it had benefited the revenue. The only difference, Walpole said, was that the word 'excise' was not used in 1723. In the event, there were other differences, and the fight against the excise scheme was the first serious attack on Walpole's policy. The attack had nothing to do with the merits of the scheme: its strength was simply a measure of the strength of the opposition, and its outcome was a measure of

Walpole's strength. The word 'excise' did provide the means of exciting opinion in the country. For excise was a hated tax, reminiscent of the long parliament, Cromwell, French absolutism and popery. Excisemen were the most detested of all the unpopular tribe of revenue officers. All this had been true in 1723. The real differences between 1723 and 1733 lay in Walpole's greatly increased stature and in Bolingbroke's activities in England. In 1723, Walpole was a prominent minister, but he was not yet a Prime Minister, towering over his colleagues: ten years later, he was the colossus, bestriding the political world, dwarfing his colleagues and, to his enemies, beginning to look immovable. Bolingbroke had now been back in England for eight years. He was pardoned in 1723 and his property was restored to him in 1725, but he was debarred from sitting in parliament and from holding office. His hope that the accession of George II might improve his political fortunes was disappointed.

In December 1726 appeared the first number of a weekly newspaper, *The Craftsman* or *Countryman*, which became the chief vehicle for opposition and patriot propaganda and remained so for the next twenty years. Its main contributors were Bolingbroke and Pulteney. Pulteney, outraged at not being offered office in 1724, trumpeted his opposition in the Commons in 1726, by a motion for a committee to enquire into the national debts. The motion was made, he said, 'with no other View than to give that Great Man an opportunity to show his Integrity to the whole World, which would finish his sublime Character'. It was defeated by 262 votes to 89. By 1730 Bolingbroke, despairing at last of getting his political disability removed while Walpole was in power, decided to concentrate single-mindedly on plans to pull Walpole down. No plan, Bolingbroke insisted, had the slightest chance of success unless based on, if not a united front opposition to Walpole, at least some degree of co-operation between Tories, led by Bolingbroke's friend Wyndham, and disappointed or discontented Whigs. Yet Tories and opposition Whigs had different aims and, looking back on their unfruitful attempts to combine, one wonders if the Tories did not lose more than they gained from following Bolingbroke's advice.

Townshend's resignation in 1730 increased the opposition, if only because it revealed something of Walpole's power in matters outside the Treasury. By 1733, Carteret stood out as Walpole's arch-opponent in the Lords. In the Commons, Pulteney was now a consistent opponent, and another Whig, the persistent Samuel Sandys, began in 1730 the series of attacks on 'the system' which earned him his nickname 'the motion maker'. He introduced four Pension Bills between 1730 and 1733: all passed the Commons, but were rejected in the Lords. In the early 1730s, Bolingbroke brought about some sort of agreement between Wyndham and Pulteney. This set the stage for the crisis.

The Excise Bill was a 'many-headed monster', attacked before it was born. Indeed, the attack was heralded in 1732 by a burst of opposition to the reintroduction of the salt tax, which was to be collected by officers of the excise. The infamous nature of an excise duty, and the terrible effects of a general excise on all commodities, were expounded in *The Craftsman* in a series of articles in the winter of 1732. They were collected and printed as *An Argument against Excises*, by Caleb D'Anvers. From then onwards, a fierce pamphlet, press and print warfare was waged. Most of the arguments against the excise scheme simply pandered to popular detestation of excise.

The present scheme, it was said, was only a first step to a general excise on all articles of consumption. The cost of living would rise, the poor would be beggared. The association of excise with the reduction of the land tax was a bribe which patriotic Englishmen would scorn to accept. Excisemen would invade

A contemporary print of Walpole (left) in the House of Commons, with the Speaker, Arthur Onslow.

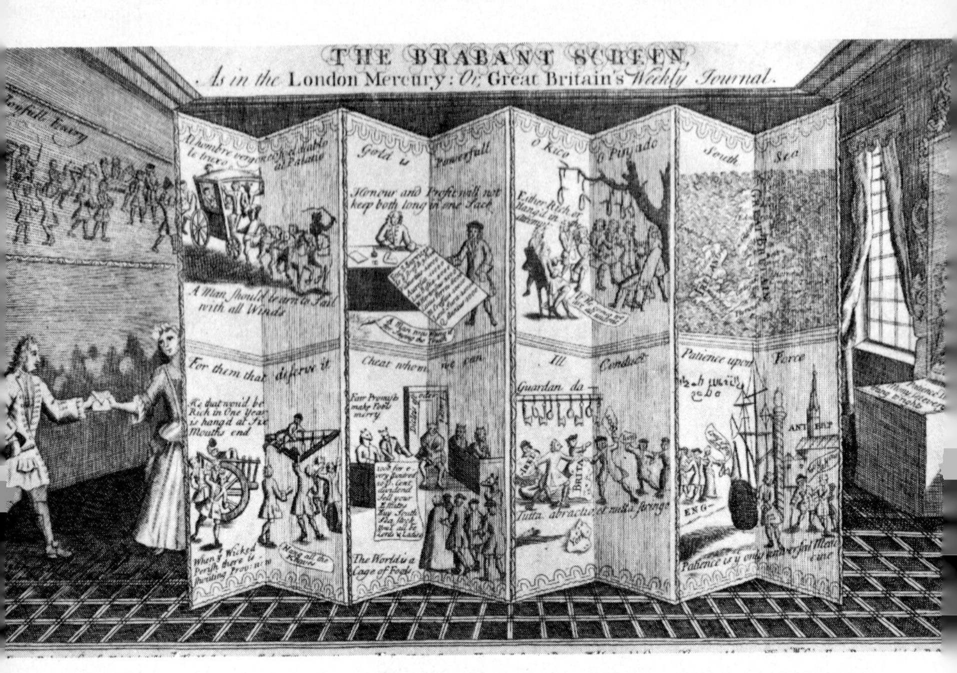

Above In eighteenth-century political lampoon the screen was a frequent symbol of deceit and concealment of the truth. *Below* The silver salver which Walpole had made by the famous silversmith Paul de Lamerie from the great seal of George I, which was given to him as Treasurer. Both the print and the central engravings on the salver are by Hogarth.

Above A cartoon castigating the highly unpopular Excise Bill of 1733. Walpole himself is caricatured as 'Excise on a Hogshead of Tobacco'.
Below A satirical print of 1737. The indignant Captain Jenkins produces his severed ear for Walpole's inspection, but Walpole refuses to see it.

Above The west front of Houghton House, designed by Colen Campbell and decorated and furnished by William Kent. *Below* The Board Room at the Old Treasury Building in Whitehall: Kent's magnificent decorations have been restored to their former glory. Both these buildings express Walpole's good taste and appreciation of fine art and architecture.

Right A cartoon depicting Britannia being cheated by a representative of one of the many dubious speculative companies that sprang up just before the South Sea Bubble crisis.

Above A vituperative piece of wishful thinking as a South Sea company director floats downwards to hell.

Horace Walpole, Robert's youngest son – connoisseur, builder of Strawberry Hill and creator of the Gothic novel.

Godfrey Kneller's elegant if somewhat flattering portrait of Walpole as first Earl of Orford and a member of the Kit-cat Club shows the art-lover rather than the bluff Norfolk squire.

This equestrian portrait of George I, by Kneller and J. Wootton, was in Walpole's own collection which was sold after his death to Catherine the Great of Russia. The picture was last heard of in the Gatchina Palace, Leningrad.

private homes at all hours of the day and night. They would destroy English liberties. An army of excisemen would be needed to collect the new duties. They would all be tools of the government. Government influence in elections would be enormously increased and would spread from the ports, where customs officers were concentrated, to all the towns and cities in the kingdom. All would be enslaved: electorate and the House of Commons they elected. The rousing slogan 'Liberty, Property, and No Excise' was born. Ballads and prints created the Excise Monster, or Dragon, devouring all things that ordinary people ate and drank.

Much of this of course was nonsense and deliberate misrepresentation. It is tempting to dismiss it, as Adam Smith did, as faction allied with self-interest: 'Faction, combined with the interest of smuggling merchants, raised so violent, though so unjust a clamour against that bill, that the minister thought proper to drop it, and from a dread of exciting a clamour of the same kind, none of his successors have dared to resume the project.' Nevertheless, though this is absolutely right, we must subdue our impatience and look at the nonsense not because we expect to find grains of sense in it, but because of its effectiveness in rousing public opinion and because of its constitutional undertones. These link it with the subsequent constitutional attack on Walpole.

In the face of certain opposition inside as well as outside parliament, Walpole decided to introduce a Bill applying only to tobacco – wines could be dealt with later. His proposal to abolish the existing duties on tobacco passed the Commons, on 14 March, by 266 votes to 205. This was a safe, though not large, majority. Three weeks later, when the Bill imposing the new duties was introduced, the motion for reading it a second time only passed by 236 votes to 200. On the day fixed for the second reading, Walpole proposed that it be postponed until 14 June. Parliament would certainly have been prorogued by then; it was in fact prorogued on

11 June. The postponement was, in effect, withdrawal. Walpole explained his reasons: it was not in the public interest to push any policy against such strong feeling in the country and a dwindling majority in the Commons. It is not certain that the Bill would actually have been defeated in the Commons. It was however undoubtedly wise not to wait and see, making defeat the touchstone for withdrawal.

Withdrawal meant, of course, that the House of Lords did not discuss the Bill. Individual peers, however, had contributed a good deal to the general tumult and had intrigued out of parliament, in particular trying to influence the King and Queen against Walpole. The Scottish peer, Stair, boasted in the House of Lords of the home truths he had told the Queen: he had told her, he said, that Walpole was like Mazarin, 'at the helm when he ought to have been rowing in the galleys'. These peers rejoiced at the withdrawal of the Bill and followed it by a surprise attack in the House of Lords, which took the form of pressure for an investigation of the affairs of the South Sea Company since 1721. On 1 June the motion for a Select Committee of enquiry was defeated by only five votes. A Protest signed by twenty-one peers condemned the defeat, which they said encouraged corruption by indicating 'a safe method of committing the most flagitious frauds under the protection of some corrupt and all-skreening minister'. This showed Walpole that he must pay attention to the House of Lords.

The King, regarding the intrigues of opposition peers who held Household offices as little short of treasonable, had dismissed the Earl of Chesterfield and Lord Clinton; this was now followed by depriving the Duke of Bolton and Lord Cobham of their regiments, and the three proud Scottish peers, Stair, Montrose and Marchmont, of their offices. More important, the government's position in the Lords was fortified by certain promotions. The most useful of these were John Hervey, Vice-Chamberlain since 1730, who was made a baron; Sir Philip Yorke, Attorney General, who became Lord Chief Justice and Baron Hardwicke; and Charles Talbot, Solicitor General, who became Lord Chancellor and Baron Talbot. The King's Speech proroguing the session referred to 'wicked Endeavours to influence the Minds of the People, and by the most unjust Misrepresentation, to raise Tumults and Disorders, that almost threaten'd the peace of the Kingdom'. No doubt Walpole composed this passage; but it certainly expressed the King's opinion.

The constitutional campaign against Walpole was fought in the next session. The two main battles, the Place Bill and the attempt to repeal the Septennial Act, began in the Commons and, like the Excise Bill, never reached the Lords. The campaign opened, however, on 13 February 1734, with a simultaneous attack in both Houses. The intention was to prevent any repetition of the reprisals which had been taken against those peers, officers in the army, who had intrigued, out of parliament, against the excise or against Walpole. The proposal was for a Bill to make army officers irremovable except by court-martial or address from both Houses of Parliament. This would have put them in the same position as the judges, an absurd parallel. Walpole, referring slyly to this proposed 'Innovation in our Constitution', wondered 'what Form of Government they aim'd at', and concluded that it must be 'a Stratocracy, an Army-Government . . . such a Government as, I believe, no Man in this Nation would be fond of'. He pointed out that the great Marlborough had been dismissed in 1711, and that his dismissal, though unwise, had not led to anything like the present proposal. The proposal was defeated in both Houses: in the Commons without a division and in the Lords by 100 votes to 62. There followed, again in both Houses, a proposal to ask the King why Bolton and Cobham had been dismissed. This was also defeated: by 252 votes to 193 in the Commons and by 77 to 48 in the Lords. The defeats in the Commons at least showed that a good many of those who had voted against the Excise Bill were not willing to vote for every move against Walpole.

These opening moves were the only ones staged simultaneously in both Houses; a lesson for the future. The main constitutional attack followed. In logic, Place Bills and proposals to repeal the Septennial Act might seem complementary: both aimed at making the House of Commons more independent of the King and the government. Logic, of course, does not always prevail: the supporters of one did not all support the other. Advocates of Place Bills argued that placemen in the House of Commons undermined its independence, and increased the power of the crown. This would, if not checked, overturn the balance of the constitution. Moreover, a placeman–member of parliament was a contradiction in terms. A man could not serve two masters; a member of parliament could not serve the King, and also the House of Commons and his constituents.

The demand for short parliaments was more complicated. It was based on an appeal to the past, on the belief that annual parliaments had once been the rule. Long parliaments, it was said, had always been docile parliaments, and docility was a sign of the King's undue influence. Charles II's Long Cavalier Parliament was quoted in support of this idea, despite the fact that it had frequently criticized the King. On the other hand, long parliaments were disliked because their members could not be controlled by their constituents: pledges could be refused, instructions could be ignored, and there was no way of calling members to account. Not everyone who disliked the Septennial Act subscribed to both these arguments. Those who did wanted a House of Commons independent in a particular way: that is, independent of the King's government but dependent, indeed tightly tied, to the electorate, or their constituents. Such a House would not be a deliberative assembly, but a legislative one. This was two stages away from Walpole's system.

The Place Bill was introduced, on 19 February, by Samuel Sandys. Its title was 'a bill for securing the Freedom of Parliament by limiting the number of Officers in that House (of Commons)'. According to its advocates, it was not an extreme measure: it is impossible to say whether they were right or wrong, for the bill did not specify the offices whose holders were to be excluded. Instead, a blank space was left, to be filled in later. By this omission it was hoped, of course, to ease the Bill's passage. Some of its supporters said that they did not wish to exclude great officers of state, or ministers, but only 'clerks in offices'. Ministers were a necessary evil: evil because they were placemen, necessary because they gave the House 'Informations'. The Bill passed its first and second readings, but was defeated by 230 votes to 191 on the motion to commit it. So the blank space was never filled in. Egmont somewhat disingenuously argued that defeat at this stage, when the Bill was 'little more than a Blank', was 'a stretch of Insolence of Power'. Walpole knew that Place Bills had always appealed to a section of the Whigs – the country Whigs, or real Whigs as they sometimes called themselves; and he was reluctant to alienate them. He did not take a prominent part in the debate, only making a short matter-of-fact speech at the end.

For him, the proposal to repeal the Septennial Act was much more important. The proposal came, on 13 March, from William Bromley, a Tory from an old Tory family. 'The people', he asserted, 'have always disliked long parliaments', and wanted to go back 'to their ancient Constitution'. Walpole was very ready to defend the Act. His defence is particularly interesting because he had been ill and not in the House when the Act was passed in 1716. The proposal was defeated right at the beginning, on the motion for leave to introduce a repealing Bill, by 247 votes to 184. It was a bigger defeat than the defeat on the Place Bill because it was defeated at an earlier stage. This fitted Walpole's order of priorities. He saw the Septennial Act as the corrector of an imbalance introduced into the constitution by the Triennial Act. The frequent elections under the Triennial Act had pushed the constitution too far in the direction of democracy, and endangered the mixture of the three pure forms of government (monarchy, aristocracy, democracy) which was the chief merit of the constitution. The Septennial Act had corrected this. It had 'brought our Constitution to a more equal Mixture, and consequently greater Perfection, than it was ever in before that Law took place'.

Walpole called this the 'serious' part of his speech. The first part consisted of a fanciful and telling reply to Wyndham's picture of an unhappy country oppressed by a 'chief Minister of State':

> Let us suppose, Sir, a Man abandoned to all Notions of Virtue and Honour, of no great Family, and of but a mean Fortune, raised to be chief Minister of State, by the Concurrence of many whimsical Events . . .
>
> Suppose him next possessed of great Wealth, the Plunder of the Nation, with a Parliament of his own chusing . . . let us suppose a Prince upon the Throne, either for want of true Information, or for some other Reason, ignorant and unacquainted with the Inclinations and the Interest of his People . . . the existence of such a Prince, or such a Minister, we cannot prevent by Act of Parliament, but the existence of such a Parliament I think we may.

Wyndham's picture was of course painted by Bolingbroke, and borrowed or copied from him. It was, Wyndham pretended, an imaginary picture. But its painter was not anonymous and Walpole did not pretend not to recognize Bolingbroke. Walpole's reply, therefore, was to paint another picture. This was more effective than taking Wyndham's picture seriously, or disputing it.

I hope that I may be allowed to draw a Picture in my Turn . . . Let us suppose, in this or in some other unfortunate Country, an Anti-Minister, who thinks himself a Person of so great and extensive Parts, and of so many eminent Qualifications, that he looks upon himself as the only Person in the Kingdom capable to conduct the publick Affairs of the Nation, and therefore christening every other Gentleman . . . by the Name of Blunderer.

The debates and outcome of the two proposals reveal the frail nature of the union of the opposition groups. The Tories could and did support both the Place Bill and the Septennial Act motion. Wyndham spoke for both, happily arguing that the Septennial Act greatly increased the need for a Place Bill, for long parliaments enabled 'a more intimate Acquaintance, and a more close Correspondence between the Crown and a Parliament, than could possibly have happened in a Course of three Years only. This is a most dangerous Novelty, which has been lately introduced.' The opposition Whigs were less happy. Country Whigs could support the Place Bill from conviction, and disaffected Whigs from a wish to defeat Walpole. They did not find it easy to support the repeal of the Septennial Act. No prominent Whigs except Pulteney and Barnard seem to have spoken. Both were brief, Barnard saying only that annual elections for City of London officials worked well. The voting figures also tell a story. Walpole's majority was larger, on both occasions, than on the second reading of the Excise Bill, and it was, as he wanted, larger on the Septennial Act motion than on the Place Bill. Surprisingly, perhaps, his majority on the Place Bill was larger in 1734 than it was in 1735, when the Bill was introduced again. With the Septennial Act, the only possible comparison is 1716: 162 voted against it then, 184 in 1734. This was not a great triumph for the opposition.

The opposition tried one more attack before the end of the

session, which was also the end of the parliament. The occasion was the debate on the King's message to both Houses on 28 March, asking for authority to increase the army and the navy should there be an emergency in the period between the dissolution and the meeting of the new parliament. In the Commons, the opposition took the unprecedented course of objecting even to Walpole's motion to take the King's message into consideration. A division was forced. Walpole's motion was carried by 211 votes to 121. On the next day, the proposal to accede to the King's request was opposed in both Houses. The voting, for Walpole, was 248 to 147 in the Commons and 101 to 58 in the Lords. The conclusion could only be that the opposition leaders over-rated both the strength and the unity of their followers. It was now clear that an attack on Walpole would not succeed, irrespective of the subject of the attack.

So, on the eve of the 1734 general election, the opposition had little to be pleased about. The policy it had attacked, the excise scheme, had been withdrawn, but not defeated in parliament, and the attacks on Walpole's system had failed. Bolingbroke, the inspirer of the parliamentary campaign as well as the campaign out of doors, knew that he had lost on both counts. Moreover, his allies had fallen out. Pulteney accused Wyndham of being nothing but Bolingbroke's puppet; Pulteney and Bolingbroke then quarrelled. The next year, Bolingbroke left England and did not return there to live until after Walpole's resignation in 1742.

The election was a hard-fought one. Great efforts were made to keep the excise scheme alive as a stick with which to beat Walpole but great efforts were made on the other side and, after all, the Bill had been withdrawn. The election gave Walpole a parliament with a majority estimated at between seventy and eighty. It was, Newcastle pronounced, 'a good parliament' – though not as good as its predecessor and apparently not as good as Walpole had hoped.

The Last Crisis 1741–2

Bolingbroke's presence may have been, as Pulteney asserted, a hindrance to the opposition in 1733–4; nevertheless, in 1741–2, without Bolingbroke, the union of opposition groups was not much deeper. Walpole was brought down, but the ministry formed after his resignation was not made out of opposition groups. Circumstances, however, were more favourable for opposition than in 1733; one must thank them, rather than any politicians or leaders, for Walpole's fall.

The timing was right, for a start. The crisis stretched over two sessions, as in 1733–4, but this time they were not the last two sessions of one parliament, but the last of one parliament and the first of the next. The general election came in the middle and not at the end of the crisis. Again, there was an attack on policy and an attack on the system, but this time they were concurrent. The policy attacked was foreign policy; and this proved even more inflammatory than the excise scheme. It was also more protracted. No one Bill was at stake, so that the attack could not be met by withdrawal. The House of Lords was involved the whole time. The attack on the system was different from the attack in 1733–4. There were two Place Bills in 1741–2, one in each session. They were the first ones to pass the Commons. There was no attempt to repeal the Septennial Act during the crisis. There was such an attempt after Walpole's fall, however, in March, when it was opposed by his successors, and defeated. In both Houses, in February 1741, there was a bitter personal attack on Walpole as Prime Minister and an attempt to force the King to dismiss him without impeaching and trying him for specific crimes or misdemeanours. This attack failed decisively in both Houses. The election in May 1741 was by no means a landslide victory for the opposition; but it left Walpole's position uncertain. If the crisis had been over, he might have been able to retrieve it, but in the middle of the crisis this was impossible. After several small defeats in the new House of Commons, and a glorious but dangerously small victory on an attack concerning policy, Walpole resigned in February 1742.

The declaration of war against Spain in October 1739 was a defeat for Walpole, or at least an abandonment of his policy of peaceful settlement, just as the withdrawal of the excise scheme had been. On both occasions, he gave in to public opinion. In 1739, however, public opinion was more widespread. 'All England', it seemed, wanted war, and 'all England' included both the King and the Prince of Wales, united in one of their rare agreements, and some at least of Walpole's colleagues. This is not to say that this united front was united also in wanting Walpole to resign. The King certainly did not want him to do so. For him, it was a question of changing policy, not a question of changing his minister; if he had to choose between them, he would choose Walpole. For Frederick, Prince of Wales, too, Walpole was more important than the policy – at all costs, he must be removed. Frederick shared the opposition view of Walpole's system and, on top of this, disliked Walpole because he was the King's minister. Frederick was the victim of a recurring pattern. After 1737 Frederick's relationship with his father deteriorated – just as George II's had done twenty years earlier – from bad terms to a public quarrel. He was expelled from St James's, established a rival court, and set out to lead the opposition. There was one difference from the 1717 pattern. Though poorer than his father had been as Prince of Wales, Frederick was more obstinate, and perhaps more principled, while his father was certainly less generous and more petty than George I had been. Partly for this reason, Walpole in office in 1742 was not able to effect a reconciliation between King and Prince, as Walpole in opposition had done in 1720.

Walpole did not pretend to like this popular Spanish war, any more than he had pretended in 1733. He bowed to public opinion, but could not pretend that his own was not better. It is, however, more difficult to pursue a policy of which one disapproves than to drop a policy of which one *does* approve. It also takes longer. Although the war began with a success, the capture of Porto Bello in the Panama Isthmus, it soon became obvious that there would be no quick, easy victory. Inevitably, Walpole was blamed. He was even blamed because the success, which was won by Admiral Vernon, a great opposition favourite, was not followed up. Though Walpole was not defeated, he was constantly harried, in both Houses, especially by the developing opposition technique of demanding papers on every conceivable negotiation with foreign powers and on every instruction to commanding officers, and then staging a debate on them.

The Place Bill introduced in January 1741 was the first of the series since 1734 to pass the Commons. This was a triumph for the opposition, and a contrast with the last four years: in January 1740, after a nine hours' debate, even the proposal to introduce a Place Bill had been defeated; and, in the preceding three years, the promoters of Place Bills did not reach even that stage. But in the Lords, at the end of February, the 1741 Bill was defeated by 63 votes to 44 on the motion to commit. There was a long Protest, signed by four peers, and subscribed, except for its last paragraph, by twenty others. It deplored the Lords' rejection of the first bill of this kind that the Commons had passed. Their passing it 'without the least Opposition', after three times rejecting similar bills, 'can only proceed either from their Conviction at last of the Necessity of such a Bill . . . or in Compliance with the almost Universal Instructions of their Constituents, whose Voice ought to have some Weight even here'.

On 13 February 1741, the day after the Place Bill passed the

Commons, there was a motion in both Houses for an Address to the King asking him to dismiss Walpole from his counsels for ever. In both Houses, it was a Whig who put the motion: Carteret in the Lords and Sandys in the Commons. Carteret's difference of opinion with Walpole was long-standing. He was interested primarily in foreign policy, and Walpole's supposed sole responsibility for it. Sandys was interested primarily in domestic affairs and Walpole's so-called unconstitutional measures. Both of them had to begin by somehow trying to justify their attempt to force the King to dismiss a minister he approved of and against whom no crime or misdemeanour had been stated. Carteret did so by the specious argument that 'common Fame' justified an Address of this kind, which, he said, was more moderate than an impeachment or act of attainder. This of course begged the question: nothing but fear of failure, and longing for quick success, restrained Walpole's opponents from impeaching him. Sandys, even more humourlessly, argued that the fact that Walpole was not being impeached exempted his opponents from naming any specific crimes or misdemeanours.

As I am only to propose an Address to remove him from his Majesty's Councils, I have no Occasion to accuse him of any Crime: The People's being generally dissatisfied with him, and suspicious of his Conduct, is a sufficient Foundation for such an Address, and a sufficient Cause for his Majesty's removing him from his Councils.

No evidence was adduced, even of the alleged dissatisfaction and suspicion. What it really amounted to was this: Walpole was a Prime Minister, so he must go.

It was stated in both Houses, quite correctly, that there was, in England, no office of 'Prime Minister', as there was in France and other countries. So, the argument went, Walpole had made for himself a position which, according to the constitution, did not exist. This position gave him undue influence over the King and, in consequence, supremacy over his colleagues and final authority for all policy, domestic and foreign. Foreign policy was examined right back to the Treaty of Hanover, for which Walpole was certainly not responsible, and large parliamentary majorities for that and for the Treaty of Seville, and even the small one for the Convention of El Pardo, were blandly ignored, or discounted as the result of corruption. Criticism of domestic policy concentrated mainly on Walpole's innovations: the excise scheme, votes of credit, the use of the sinking fund for current expenditure, even, absurdly enough, the reduction of the land tax. None of these arguments hid the personal attack on Walpole.

In the Commons, Walpole made his own defence. It was sensible, moderate, at times ironical and forceful. He denied that he was a Prime Minister, and he denied sole responsibility for foreign policy, which had, he rightly said, been approved by large majorities in both Houses. He accused his opponents of simply wanting to get him out and themselves in. He condemned their way of trying to do so, by Address to the King, as a gross invasion of the King's prerogative. Walpole's speech is a superb example of his skill in mingling orderly and reasonable argument with rhetoric. No wonder it made a deep impression on the House! It was a long speech, whose main content was a clear and comprehensive survey of the principles of foreign and domestic policy for the past twenty years. A few sentences will illustrate the reflections on his own position and on that of his opponents, with which the survey was interspersed.

But my great and principal crime is, my long continuance in office, or, in other words, the long exclusion of those who now complain against me. . . . I will not attempt to deny the reasonableness and necessity of a party war; but in carrying on that war, all principles and rules of justice should not be departed from. . . . In party contests, why should not both sides be equally steady? . . . Why is not principle the cement of one as well as the other? . . . Have gentlemen produced one instance of this exorbitant power, of the influence which I extend to all parts of the nation, of the tyranny with which I oppress those who oppose, and the liberality with which I reward those who support me? But, having first invested me with a kind of mock dignity, and styled me a prime minister, they impute to me an unpardonable abuse of that chimerical authority, which they only have created and conferred. If they are really persuaded that the army is annually established by me, that I have the sole disposal of posts and honours, that I employ this power in the destruction of liberty, and the diminution of commerce, let me awaken them from their delusion.

Walpole dominated the debate. Moreover, agreement with his view of the personal nature of the attack and with his argument about the invasion of the prerogative affected the outcome. Dissentient Whigs and country Whigs voted against him. But many Tories did not – their conduct, Bolingbroke said, was 'silly, infamous, and devoid of any colour of excuse'. Some stayed away. Twenty-five or so, including the able, independent Henry Hyde, known as Lord Cornbury, voted for Walpole. Shippen and thirty-four of his friends, so-called Jacobites, walked out in protest against this 'scheme for turning out one minister, and bringing in another', and about twenty other Tories joined them. The proposal was defeated by 290 votes to 106. The defeat would have been a serious one at any time; in the circumstances, and considering that everything depended on co-operation between Tories and dissentient Whigs, it was shattering.

Nothing could have been a greater tribute to Walpole. His triumph was celebrated in a print, *The Motion*, which began a two-year pictorial propaganda war of prints and counter-prints. At last, this very effective form of popular propaganda was used for, as well as against, Walpole. It was too late. The 'corruption *versus* independence' theme was too well established. It was simple, appealing, moral, and in the same vein of 'black *versus* white' as the country *versus* court prints of Exclusion Bill days.

In the Lords, too, the defeat of the motion was decisive. The voting was 59 for it, 108 against. Again, as with the Place Bill, a Protest was entered. It was generally supposed that Bolingbroke drafted it. Certainly it expressed his sentiments.

Because we are persuaded that a sole, or even a first Minister is an Officer unknown to the Law of *Britain*, inconsistent with the Constitution of this Country, and destructive of Liberty in any Government whatsoever; and it plainly appearing to us that Sir *Robert Walpole* has for many Years acted, as such, by taking upon himself the chief, if not the sole Direction of Affairs, in the different Branches of the Administration, we could not but esteem it to be our indispensible Duty, to offer our most humble Advice to his Majesty, for the Removal of a Minister so dangerous to the King and the Kingdoms.

A counter-resolution proposed by Marlborough, grandson of the great Duke, ran: 'That any attempt to inflict any kind of punishment on any person without allowing him an Opportunity to make his Defence, or without any Proof of any Crime or Misdemeanor committed by him, is contrary to natural justice'. It passed without a division.

The defeat of Sandys's motion was a great personal triumph for Walpole, as was the defeat of the Peerage Bill in 1719 and the defeat of the Septennial Act motion in 1734. All three were constitutional issues, mixed to a greater or lesser extent with personal ones. There had been other triumphs, and indeed there were others to come, but these were perhaps the greatest. In 1719 King, ministers, and House of Lords had been arrayed against him; in 1734, in the aftermath of his abandonment of an unpopular policy, he met an attempt to repeal an Act which he considered vital to the working of the constitution; in 1741, he faced an alliance which, if it held, would defeat him. On all three occasions he showed personal qualities which put him in the very front rank of leaders: courage, tenacity, seriousness of purpose, the determination to lift the debate above the personal issues that depended on it, and the ability to do so. In 1741, he could not ignore the personal charges against him, and he answered them composedly and convincingly. The 'eloquence', 'vivacity' and 'animation', upon which his contemporaries so often remarked, are so apparent in his speeches on these three occasions that one wonders why posterity has not often used these phrases of him. Perhaps it has listened too much to his opponents.

Beyond this, the comparison of 1719, 1734 and 1741 invites a question: had Walpole's views about the constitution changed between 1719 and 1741? Did he think his long ascendancy had changed the constitution; or think that it had shown the way to make the constitution work? It seems clear from Walpole's speeches in 1734 and in 1741 that he did not think his 1719 views were out-of-date. That is, he believed that his practice was compatible with the idea of balance as he had expounded it in 1719. Indeed, he believed that this practice was what made the balance work.

The victory of February 1741 made it clear that, if Walpole were to be defeated, it would not be on a motion of this kind. Nevertheless, the victory could not possibly end the crisis. An election was due and parliament was dissolved in April. The election was a triumph neither for Walpole, nor for his opponents; for the new House of Commons was very evenly divided. Dodington called it 'the most equally balanced parliament that ever was returned'. A great deal therefore depended on the kind of attack made on him in the new parliament. Personal attacks were unlikely to succeed, and attacks on the system were perhaps no more likely to succeed than in the past. Attacks on policy might be met by a change of policy rather than Walpole's resignation. Attacks on trivial matters, apparently not connected with Walpole at all, might be more effective, for they would give Walpole no chance to defend himself, nor to attract the sort of support that he seemed always able to win on great occasions.

Walpole was faced with a series of such attacks as soon as parliament met on 1 December 1741. The occasions were not connected either with policy or, on the face of it, with Walpole's position. They were simply routine, beginning-of-parliament occasions: the Address in reply to the King's Speech, the election of the chairman of the Committee of Privileges and Elections, the trial of disputed elections.

The proposed Address in reply to the King's Speech was challenged in both Houses. By now, the King's Speech was 'well known to be the Composition of the Ministry' and criticism of the proposed Address in reply to it therefore an opposition tactic. The usual complaint, voiced many times by Shippen, was that the modern form of the Address was not just a general expression of thanks to the King, but mentioned all the points in the Speech. Shippen argued that this deceived the ordinary man, who did not understand how parliament worked, into thinking that the whole House approved everything that ministers had done or proposed to do. The complaint was, on this occasion, made in the House of Lords, where Chesterfield proposed that thanks be given 'in general terms, according to the ancient Practice of this House'. His proposal was defeated by eighty-eight votes to forty-three. In the Commons, a rather different proposal was made. It was to omit from the Address the particular clause thanking the King for his care in prosecuting the war against Spain. This implied criticism of Walpole was agreed to without a division. Pulteney, who had seconded the proposal, then moved for a Committee of the Whole House to consider the State of the Nation. Walpole answered this by seconding Pulteney's motion. The day fixed for the Committee to meet was 21 January.

The other two attacks on Walpole at the beginning of the new parliament concerned elections and were therefore made only in the House of Commons. Dr George Lee, a Tory, stood for election as Chairman of the Committee of Privileges and Elections against Giles Erle, who had been Chairman in the last two parliaments and was proposed by Walpole. Lee was elected by 242 votes to 238. This was the first of the series of tiny minorities, and tiny majorities, that showed how evenly the new parliament was divided.

The trial of disputed elections provided further evidence of this. The right to try and decide disputed elections had belonged to the House of Commons since 1604, and was regarded as a vital part of its control over its own members. In 1704, after the Aylesbury controversy, the House extended its power to include the right to decide the qualifications of voters. Walpole had unsuccessfully opposed this extension. By 1742, it was well known that the decisions made about disputed elections at the beginning of a parliament were indications of the relative strength of ministers and their opponents. The decisions also affected that relative strength, and this was particularly important in the kind of parliament just elected. In 1742, there were more disputed elections than usual. The most important was Westminster, where there had been riots and the local magistrates had had to call in soldiers. The trial was on 22 December. The decision went against the two sitting members, supporters of Walpole, by four and five votes respectively. Parliament then adjourned over Christmas. At this time, Walpole was not well. His attempt to increase his support by effecting a reconciliation between the King and the Prince of Wales failed because the Prince refused to consider reconciliation while Walpole remained in power. When parliament met again on 18

January, another disputed election, Berwick, was decided against Walpole's supporters.

Three days later, on 21 January, another Place Bill was introduced. On the same day, which had been fixed for the Committee on the State of the Nation, Pulteney made a surprise attack. He proposed that the papers relating to the war should not be considered by the whole House, but should first be referred to a select committee. This was a serious attack, far more dangerous than questions of disputed elections. The proposed method was new, and Pulteney's committee would of course have consisted of Walpole's opponents. The proposal was defeated, in an exceptionally large House, by the narrow majority of 253 votes to 250.

This was another of Walpole's magnificent victories: but it was too narrow. A majority of three, in the middle of a war, was unworkable, an impossible strain. All Walpole's friends, except the King, thought he should resign; the King begged him not to. On 31 January, Walpole made his decision. On 1 February, another disputed election decision, Chippenham, went against him, this time by sixteen votes. On 3 February, both Houses adjourned, by the King's request, and on 11 February Walpole resigned. On 17 February, Frederick, Prince of Wales, waited on the King 'after several Years' Absence from Court' and a 'happy Reconciliation' followed.

Walpole's resignation was in accordance with his professions: he had been chosen by the King, but kept in office by the confidence of the House of Commons. He resigned, against the King's wishes, because he had lost that confidence. He had not been defeated either by a large majority or on any important issue: neither on policy, nor on a straight 'Walpole or not Walpole' question. Perhaps he never would have been.

The disputed election defeats, and even the defeat on the Committee of Privileges and Elections, were small. Literally, they were not defeats for Walpole at all, though they were certainly defeats for his wishes. The victory of only three votes on Pulteney's motion was a much more important indication that Walpole's long ascendancy had gone. His resignation created the rule that ministers who lost the support of the House of Commons must resign, or, to put it the other way round, that the House of Commons could force ministers to resign. It became a rule of prime importance in English political life for more than a century and was only undermined when a dissolution became an acceptable alternative to resignation: one can hardly put this before 1867. The rule was also undermined in practice after 1867 when the new form of two-party system made it unlikely that any government, chosen now at the same time as the House of Commons, and therefore having the same party colouring, would be defeated in the Commons.

Few precedents in politics have ever become a rule as quickly as this one of Walpole's did. In its immediate context, it implied that the King's favour was not, and ought not to be, enough to keep a minister in power. At the same time, the decision to resign, or to dismiss, lay with the minister, or the King, and not with the two Houses as it would have done if Sandys's motion had passed the Commons, and Carteret's the Lords, in February 1741. The resignation also implied that the support of the Commons, not the support of parliament as a whole, was the vital factor in a minister's power. In a way this is surprising, for the House of Lords had played a vigorous part in the hunting of Walpole. But his resignation removed any possibility or need of using impeachment as a weapon against ministers, to force resignation or dismissal; it was never used in this way again. This took from the House of Lords their right to try ministers impeached by the Commons and so, in effect, to make the final decision. The attempt to impeach Walpole after his resignation only underlines this. It was as if the opposition, not quite able to accept what had happened, tried to reassure themselves by appealing to the Lords and asserting that Walpole had, after all, been guilty of punishable crimes. The investigating committee's efforts to discover these crimes failed, and the impeachment of course was never brought. If it had been, Walpole's rule, as it might be called, would not have been made.

Two Sides

In terms of practical politics, there were not in Walpole's time two sides led by two leaders. In the crises of 1733–4 and 1741–2 Walpole faced opposition, but he did not face an opposition party. There was no leader of the opposition, nor even a single acknowledged rival for power. There was no duel like the Pitt–Fox duel at the end of the century; still less was there anything resembling the Gladstone–Disraeli duel in the second half of the nineteenth century. In terms of theory, however, there were two sides. Walpole was not merely 'a great practical politician'; he was a statesman who theorized. There is a great deal of theory both in his speeches and in his pamphlets. This theory was not just a repetition of current platitudes or generally accepted notions; it would have a place in any study of eighteenth-century political ideas even if Walpole had not been prominent in political practice. But of course his ideas are doubly interesting – from the Aylesbury controversy in 1704, Sacheverell's impeachment in 1710, and the Peerage Bill in 1719, down to his rejoinders to the criticism of his own position in the 1730s – because of their bearing on his practice.

The two sides may, for the sake of convenience, be labelled Walpole's and Bolingbroke's. Like all labels, these two are misleading if taken quite literally, and of course, on both sides, not all the theories were expressed by the principals. But to replace the label 'Bolingbroke's' by 'anti-Walpole' might be more misleading because it would imply that this side was later in time than Walpole's and concerned simply with refuting him.

The basic division between the two sides was their different interpretation of the Glorious Revolution and of the principles of 1689. Walpole of course approved those principles and one must believe that Bolingbroke did also.

The principles of 1689, in this particular context, meant a mixed constitution, containing elements of the three pure, or simple, forms of constitution – monarchy, aristocracy, and democracy – without leaning to any one of the three. The mixture was made concrete in the tripartite division of parliament, the supreme law-making body. King, Lords and Commons formed a balance of power, a trinity, not a unitary power. This division of power prevented tyranny and preserved freedom. None of the three parts of parliament could act alone and the body they jointly constituted could only act if all three were agreed.

If there was agreement over this, there was also sharp disagreement about the relationship of the three parts of the balance. Did balance mean that the three parts of the trio were, or should be, equal in power? Did it require each of them to be separate and independent of the other two? Most of those who thought the three partners ought to be equal feared that the King was becoming too strong for his partners; in particular, they feared his influence over the House of Commons. They therefore advocated Place Bills to keep out of the Commons men connected with the King. A few feared that the Commons, rather than the King, might become too strong and therefore welcomed placemen as a brake on their power. The argument about separation and independence went along the same lines. Those who advocated the independence of the House of Commons wanted to forbid members of parliament from holding places or pensions because these represented pieces of the King's influence, the King intruding into the Commons and undermining its independence. Those who advocated the independence of the House of Lords saw the King's prerogative of creating peers at will as a danger, and so supported the Peerage Bill which would have limited this prerogative. Opponents of Place Bills and the Peerage Bill believed that separation and independence would simply create three antagonistic parts of parliament. The result would be either stalemate or civil war. They did not, however, oppose separation and independence only on practical grounds. They also opposed on principle.

Walpole both stated and acted his position on these questions. In the debate on the Peerage Bill, and in his pamphlet *Thoughts of a Member of the Lower House*, he argued for a balanced constitution based on three dependent, not independent parts. He objected to the Peerage Bill because it would make the Lords independent of King and Commons, the other two parts of parliament. If the bill were to be passed, he wrote,

> The House of Lords will be a fixed independent Body, not to be called to account like a Ministry, not to be dissolved and changed like a House of Commons . . . [The Bill puts] King and Ministry entirely at the mercy of the Lords, and makes the Commons more dependent on the Crown.

He rejected, at least by implication, any idea of equality of the three powers. He opposed the Peerage Bill because it would work to the detriment of the Commons; the Lords' gain in power would be the Commons' loss. The Commons would not lose if the King kept his power of creating peers; indeed, they would probably benefit from it. The benefit was rather different from anything that Walpole could have imagined. In 1832, and again 1911, the Lords, rather than suffer a creation of peers like Anne's, surrendered to the threat of it. Really, of course, this benefited the government which made the threat, rather than the House of Commons.

In his opposition to Place Bills, Walpole used the practical rather than the theoretical argument. He was defending a particular kind of government, and he believed it would not work if the three parts of parliament were independent and separate. That kind of government depended on a link between the King's ministers and the House of Commons. This link would not weaken the Commons; separation would do that. This was most obvious in the sphere of finance. The Commons had the power to vote or refuse supply. It would be folly to exclude from the Commons the ministers, junior ministers, and secretaries responsible both for requesting supply and for suggesting ways of raising it. The same was true, perhaps to a lesser extent, of foreign affairs and other spheres of activity. Places of other kinds, which had nothing to do with the working of government, might be regarded as cement to hold government supporters together. They were rewards, or a help towards election expenses, not bribes. They were a very loose cement. This was a reasonably true picture of patronage. The point, however, is not the truth of the picture but the fact that Walpole believed that a connection between King's ministers and Commons was vital. Independence, in the sense of absence of connection, could only foster the sort of friction that led to civil war. Bishop Sherlock stated this as an axiom in 1731:

That whatever tends to break the Balance between the Powers essential to this Constitution, must sooner or later prove to be the ruin of the Whole. That an independent House of Commons, or an independent House of Lords, was as inconsistent with our Constitution, as an independent, that is absolute King. That whoever loves the Liberties and Laws of his Country, would no more desire to see the one than the other.

With the debate on the proposal to repeal the Septennial Act in 1734, Walpole came back to theory. The Septennial Act was, he contended, the guarantee of the mixed constitution and, therefore, of the principles of 1689. After his quick and clever picture of an Anti-Minister, to demolish Wyndham's picture of 'a Man . . . of no great Family, and of but a mean Fortune, raised to be the chief Minister of State, by the Concurrence of many whimsical Events', Walpole turned 'to be serious, and to talk really to the Subject in hand'. This subject was the constitution.

The nature of our Constitution seems to be very much mistaken by the Gentlemen who have spoken in favour of this Motion. It is certain, that ours is a mixt Government, and the Perfection of our Constitution consists in this, that the Monarchical, Aristocratical and Democratical Forms of Government are mixt and interwoven in ours, so as to give us the Advantages of each, without subjecting us to the Dangers and Inconveniences of either. . . .

This, Sir, would in my opinion be our Misfortune, if our Parliaments were either Annual or Triennial. By such frequent Elections, there would be so much Power thrown into the Hands of the People, as would destroy that equal Mixture, which is the Beauty of our Constitution: In short, our Government would really become a Democratical Government and might from thence very probably diverge into a tyrannical. Therefore, in order to preserve our Constitution, in order to prevent our falling under Tyranny and Arbitrary Power, we ought to preserve that Law, which I really think has brought our Constitution to a more equal Mixture, and consequently greater Perfection than it was ever in before that Law took place.

The Bolingbroke position challenged Walpole's on all counts, and the challenge was all the more bitter because Bolingbroke supposedly agreed with Walpole on the merits of a mixed and balanced constitution. They did not, however, agree on the relation of this constitution to the Glorious Revolution. Bolingbroke believed that this kind of constitution and liberty had existed in England from time immemorial. It could be found in the Anglo-Saxon assembly, the Witanagemot. The Revolution confirmed it, perhaps, or restored it, after the upsets brought by the Stuart Kings, particularly James II. Walpole's side did not see the Revolution as restoration. Walpole believed that the Revolution had established a new kind of constitution; for the first time, Englishmen now had a mixed, balanced constitution, guarantee of liberty.

For my part [said Thomas Robinson in the debate on the repeal of the Septennial Act in 1734], I do not understand what is meant by our old Constitution . . . I know of no settled Constitution till the Revolution: 'tis from that happy Period I date our having any at all. . . . Gentlemen . . . on the other side of the Question, make a very partial use of our ancient Constitution, when they plead for a shorter Duration of Parliament. . . . Would [they] have our Parliaments brought again to be entirely on the same Foot as formerly? Surely, No!

This difference of opinion about English history was fundamental. Walpole, according to modern scholarship, had the better opinion. Bolingbroke was wrong about the Anglo-Saxons, and about the Witanagemot, which was not a democratic assembly. This is an interesting little sidelight. But what matters is the structure erected on the two theories. Bolingbroke's theory led him to talk about the superiority of 'the people' to the House of Commons. Sovereignty, he said, lay in the people, not in parliament. Therefore, members of parliament were delegates of their constituents and should be bound by commands and instructions issued by them. These ideas about representation were strongly contested by Walpole and his supporters. Again, it was the proposal for the repeal of the Septennial Act which brought out the controversy. Willes, one of Walpole's supporters, defined the relation between members of parliament and their constituents as Burke was to define it later: 'representation' as opposed to 'delegation'.

That we have all a Dependence upon the People for our Election is what, Sir, I shall readily grant; but after we are chosen, and have taken our Seats in this House, we have no longer any Dependence on our Electors, at least in so far as regards our Behaviour here: Their whole Power is then devolved upon us, and we are in every Question that comes before this House, to regard only the publick Good in General, and to determine according to our own Judgments . . . if we are to depend upon our Representatives, and to follow blindly the Instructions they send us, we cannot be said to act freely, nor can such Parliaments be regarded as free Parliaments.

Bolingbroke's ideas about representation also led him to insist on the merits of short parliaments and annual, or at least triennial, general elections. This would enable constituents frequently to judge the conduct of their members and to change them if their conduct had been unsatisfactory. The Septennial Act should be repealed and a return made to the happy days of the old constitution when parliaments were elected each year. Long parliaments freed members from their constituents and led members to think about ministers instead of only about their constituents. This opened the door to what Bolingbroke called 'corruption'.

By 'corruption', Bolingbroke's side meant loss of independence. It came from association between ministers and members and the acceptance of places by members. As Sir John St Aubyn said in 1734, supporting the repeal of the Septennial Act: 'A further mischief of long Parliaments is, that a Minister has Time and opportunities of getting Acquaintance with Members, of practising his several Arts to win them into his Schemes.' For Bolingbroke, the balance of the constitution meant that the three parts of parliament, King, Lords and Commons, should be independent of each other and roughly equal in power.

> In a Constitution like ours [Bolingbroke wrote in *Remarks on the History of England*] the safety of the whole depends on the balance of the parts, and the balance of the parts consists in their mutual independency on each other. The independency pleaded for consists in this; that the resolutions of each part, which direct these proceedings, be taken independently and without any influence, direct or indirect, on the others.

The Protest against the rejection of the 1741 Place Bill by the Lords echoed this:

> Because we conceive, that our Constitution itself points out this Bill, as one of its principal Securities; a due Poize and Independency of the three several Constituent Parts of the Supreme Legislative Power, being required by the Spirit of our Constitution, and absolutely necessary to its existence. If any one of these becomes dependent on the other, the Constitution is dangerously altered.

This was not the same as separation of powers, soon to be enshrined by Montesquieu as the recipe for a free state. Montesquieu's three powers were functional: executive, legislative, and judicative. Bolingbroke's were institutional: King, Lords, and Commons. The Commons must be freed from the King's influence by forbidding its members to hold crown offices. This meant Place Bills.

It also meant that there must be no Prime Minister. A Prime Minister was the instrument of 'corruption': it was he who enslaved the Commons by distributing places to its members. He was also the beneficiary of 'corruption'. A free House of Commons would not, Bolingbroke asserted, support Walpole's policy. Here, too, there was an argument drawn from history. In the past, it was said, ministers had been equal, each of them keeping within his own sphere of activity and directly responsible to the monarch for the conduct of it. A Prime Minister was a King's favourite. He held one particular office of state, but did not confine himself to the work proper to that office; therefore, he obtained an improper hold over his colleagues and over all branches of policy. It was of course also argued that Walpole's policy was bad. Therefore he must be got rid of. But the fundamental objection was that the policy was his and, it was said, his alone. The remedy lay not in finding a better Prime Minister with a better policy, but in doing without a Prime Minister and returning to what was sometimes called departmental government.

This was, in practice, a convenient theory in the 1730s, for the opposition could certainly not have produced an alternative Prime Minister. The wish to do without one shows a complete and wilful misunderstanding of Walpole's position. It also shows such a sad degree of nostalgic romanticism, or escapism, that it becomes the least serious and least acceptable part of Bolingbroke's creed. Ministers could be equal if the monarch were the active head of the executive. This had been so, perhaps, in the reign of Bolingbroke's favourite monarch, Elizabeth. It had also been true in the reign of a more recent monarch, less favoured by Bolingbroke, William III. No one wished the Hanoverians to be monarchs of that kind. Or did Bolingbroke really think it possible that Frederick, Prince of Wales, might be welcomed as a patriot King, a king without parties and without a Prime Minister? To offer a patriot King as a remedy for Prime Ministers and 'corruption' was either a confession of failure, or utopian, or both. It seemed, to Burke, worse than this.

Burke's contempt of Bolingbroke had other roots. He disliked Bolingbroke's theory of representation. He detested his views about party. These views of course went within the idea of the patriot

King. The original 'real' party divisions, the Whigs and Tories of the 1680s, Bolingbroke argued, disappeared in 1689: both parties then lost their *raison d'être*. The division that existed in the 1730s was therefore not a division between two parties but simply a division between the constitutionalists, Bolingbroke's side, and the anti-constitutionalists, Walpole's side. Walpole's supporters were not a real party: they were a faction, held together not by principles but by places and pensions. The other side, the constitutionalists, were not really a party either. That is, they were a 'national party' – a contradiction in terms – a party of patriots, with no object but the general good of the nation and the restoration of the constitution. The constitution had been perverted by Walpole as, before 1689, it had been perverted by the Stuarts. The difference was that the Stuarts had been wicked kings, while the Hanoverians were weak kings, duped and led astray by Walpole. Burke rejected all these ideas.

Though many of Bolingbroke's ideas are backward-looking, they are not for that reason to be written off as impracticable, or utopian. Bolingbroke poured scorn on the word 'utopian'. In 1730, a rash writer in the *London Journal* had argued that 'the carrying on of business, and maintaining government by powers absolutely distinct, and absolutely independent, is a mere Utopian scheme.' This, said Bolingbroke, 'must proceed from ignorance or folly'. It is not, perhaps, much in the way of proof, especially as the other side put forward arguments based on principle as well as on practicability. Nevertheless, perhaps the utopian argument is an unfair one, and too easy a way of dismissing Bolingbroke's ideas. What would these ideas have done? They would have produced a totally different House of Commons, and a totally different kind of executive government. The Commons would have been cut off from ministers and junior ministers. It would, as a body, have lacked cohesion and predictability. It would have been a body of delegates, not part of a sovereign body. Its function would have been not deliberative but legislative, and it would presumably have legislated in accordance with a programme decided on before it was elected. Such a body would have been weaker, not stronger, than the existing one. There would have been no Prime Ministers; ministers would have been equal. Perhaps, after all, a constitution like this would have needed a patriot King.

This picture deepens our understanding of Walpole's ideas, and brings us back to the novelty of his practice. For he wished to avoid all these things not in the interests of so-called corruption or crown influence, but in the interests of a working constitution which required, as its basis, a connection between all three parts of parliament. There can be no doubt that the Commons benefited from not becoming 'independent' in the Bolingbroke way, just as it benefited from not having the Septennial Act repealed and from having its greatest member as the King's chief minister. This perhaps means also that Bolingbroke was wrong in thinking that the balance of the constitution must rest on the independence of its three parts. It was Bolingbroke's reforms, not Walpole's, that would have upset the balance.

6
AFTERMATH

1742–5

Walpole's resignation in February 1742 was as dramatic as Peel's just over a century later. Both men were attacked by an ephemeral combination of groups which had nothing in common except their attack. If Walpole looks less heroic than Peel, it is because he never played the hero. Yet his fall was a personal tragedy, or drama, just as Peel's was; and he deserves the same sort of sympathy accorded to Peel. He was hounded quite as mercilessly, and for a much longer period. Walpole's speeches in the two years before his resignation show that, like Peel, he could rise to heights of eloquence and speak generalities, as well as give lucid expositions of facts and figures. He had shown this before, on great occasions: in 1719 and 1734 for example. There is a new note towards the end: it is not the impatience and indeed contempt that Peel showed, of a man goaded beyond reason; rather, it is the occasional sharpness of an equable man who, in spite of himself, has let himself see that he is being unjustly treated.

If my whole administration is to be scrutinised and arraigned [he objected in 1741] why are the most favourable parts to be omitted? If facts are to be accumulated on one side, why not on the other? And why may not I be permitted to speak in my own favour? [and replying to attacks on foreign policy] Admitting, however, for the sake of argument, that I am prime and sole minister in this country; am I, therefore, prime and sole minister of all Europe?

Drama apart, Walpole's resignation was far and away more shattering. It raised fundamental constitutional questions as well as political and party ones. Peel was bound to be followed by another Prime Minister; Walpole was not so bound. Would there now, as some of his jubilant opponents hoped, be no more Prime Ministers? Would Walpole's 'system' end with him? Opponents of 'Prime Ministers' and 'the system' were however not the strongest part of the coalition against Walpole – that part was made up of disaffected Whigs, led by Pulteney and Carteret, whose wish was to step into Walpole's shoes, not to discard them. They did not do so. For one thing, none of them had Walpole's ascendancy in the Commons. (Pulteney, who had a lesser sway, could perhaps only sustain it in opposition; anyhow he threw it away and became a peer.) For another, George II, though attracted by Carteret's ideas on foreign policy, knew that his advice in general was less wise than Walpole's, whose last advice to the King, in November 1744, was to dismiss Carteret, as most of his other ministers wanted. As far as the King was concerned, therefore, one part of being a Prime Minister, advising the King generally, remained with Walpole until he died in March 1745. Indeed, that part died with Walpole, for George II never again had a minister whom he relied on to the same extent.

Two days before Walpole resigned, he at last accepted a peerage. His retirement from the House of Commons, which he had dominated for so long, signified, without a doubt, retirement from active politics and from political ambition. He took the title Earl of Orford, the name of his Chelsea house which had previously been occupied by Edward Russell, Earl of Orford, one of the Whig Junto lords who had been unsuccessfully impeached, in 1701, by a

Tory House of Commons. Walpole had worked with Orford and been friendly with him. It might be tempting to see Walpole's choice of title as a piece of symbolism, or a bit of bravado, on the part of a fallen minister who knew that his enemies were longing to impeach him. But it may have been simply that he had always liked the house, and had begun his ministerial career there in 1715.

The attempt to impeach Walpole was a miserable affair. Luckily for their own reputation, the new ministers did not wholeheartedly support it. The first proposal, to enquire into Walpole's conduct for the last twenty years, was defeated. The next proposal, for an enquiry covering the last ten years, was successful. However, the investigating committee could find nothing which would remotely justify bringing an impeachment and it therefore suggested that witnesses should be free to 'disclose and discover, to the best of their knowledge, remembrance, and belief' anything about Walpole's conduct, without incriminating themselves. A Bill embodying this extraordinary suggestion was passed by the House of Commons, in spite of strenuous opposition, by 228 votes to 216. It was rejected by the Lords by 109 votes to 57. Carteret joined with Newcastle and Hardwicke to denounce its absurdity and injustice. A Commons resolution condemning the conduct of the Lords was defeated. The committee reported; but the report, though vindictive, could hardly lead to impeachment. An attempt to revive the investigation in December 1743 was defeated. By that time, many of Walpole's opponents were finding the new ministry as bad as the old. Walpole attended the House of Lords, but not often. His only recorded speech was in February 1744, when he chided the Lords for not responding more vigorously to the King's message about the Pretender's preparations for invasion.

Ministers, as well as the King, continued to consult Walpole. Most of the ministers were, in fact, Walpole's ministers. George II wrote to Pulteney hoping that he 'would not distress the government by making too many [ministerial] changes in the midst of the session'. For one reason and another, there were very few changes. Pulteney discussed them with Newcastle and Hardwicke, and the only one of any importance, apart from the replacement of Walpole at the Treasury, was Carteret's appointment as Secretary of State. Pulteney, apparently by his own wish, went to the House of Lords as Earl of Bath, but took no office. The Tories got nothing in the way of offices except the Privy Seal for Earl Gower. Walpole was replaced as First Lord of the Treasury by the Earl of Wilmington, the Spencer Compton who had been poised to replace him in 1727; and as Chancellor of the Exchequer by Samuel Sandys. The arrangement did not last long. Wilmington died in August 1743 and Pulteney, regretting that he had not taken an office as well as a peerage in 1742, asked to succeed him. He was refused. Against Carteret's wishes, but in accordance with Walpole's, Wilmington was succeeded by Henry Pelham, Walpole's right-hand financial man. In December, Sandys resigned and went to the Lords. Pelham then took over his office of Chancellor of the Exchequer. Walpole's other ministers remained: Hardwicke as Lord Chancellor, Devonshire as Lord Privy Seal, and Newcastle as Secretary of State (the other Secretary of State, Harrington, became Lord President of the Council to make way for Carteret). Although this lasted a little longer than the Treasury rearrangements, Carteret went out and Harrington came back in November 1744.

So, before Walpole died, the three new ministers were all out again, and his pupil and close follower, Henry Pelham, was at the Treasury, combining the offices of First Lord and Chancellor as Walpole had done. Pelham eventually managed the House of Commons, but he never quite towered above it as Walpole had done. He managed his colleagues, too, but he did not master them: instead, he tried to muzzle potential critics by including them in the ministry. He was an able financier, controlling the Treasury and all domestic affairs, but his authority in foreign affairs was much weaker than Walpole's. This was partly because his handling of his brother, Newcastle, was less adroit than Walpole's had been, but mainly because Pelham was not interested in foreign policy, which he regarded as unduly expensive and a distraction from financial policy.

The Next Century

Walpole did not have to wait long for appreciation or rehabilitation. Even in the year he resigned, David Hume gave one reason why the Great Man could now be praised. He had been brought down after staying twenty years in power, and during at least ten of those years he had seemed proof against all assaults. So Hume added a qualifying note to his *Character of Walpole* before it was published in 1742:

> The character of *Sir Robert Walpole* was drawn some months ago, when that Great Man was in the Zenith of his Power. I must confess, when he seems to be on the Decline, I am inclin'd to think more favourably of him, and to suspect, that the Antipathy, which every true born *Briton* naturally bears to Ministers of State, inspir'd me with some Prejudice against him.

Another reason why people began to think favourably of Walpole after his resignation lay in the shortcomings of his immediate successors. Carteret's conduct of the war was vigorous but not highly successful, and his policy was more, not less, 'Hanoverian' than Walpole's. The French refusal to expel the Pretender in 1744, and the Jacobite rebellion in 1745, proved that Walpole had been right to insist that Jacobitism, especially in the form of French help to the Pretender, was still a danger. The constitution was not remade. Carteret seemed bent on being a 'sole' minister, at least in the sense of King's favourite, and he was a more distasteful one than Walpole, because he was more arrogant. Pulteney's patriotism waned, and was no longer believed in. A Place Bill introduced in April passed both Houses, but did not satisfy its promoters. The taste for Place Bills was deep amongst Tories and certain country Whigs, and yet another was introduced in December. Walpolians might be expected to oppose it, but it was hard that its chief opponent should be motion-maker Sandys. He opposed it on the incredible grounds that the new ministers had not yet had time to explain to the King how desirable Place Bills were. A motion to repeal the Septennial Act, in March 1742, was opposed by the new ministers as strongly as Walpole had opposed it in 1734, though with less consistency. It was defeated by 209 votes to 184. The size of the minority was exactly the same as in 1734. Tories could hardly see these post-Walpole happenings as an improvement on Walpole.

Walpole's reputation gained by these failings. It gained too from his generous and optimistic temperament. The fact that Walpole seldom took offence, never sulked, did not stand upon his dignity, and was, as Pulteney said, 'hard to be provoked', must be a merit in him rather than in his opponents. He could be clever at their expense, for example in 1734, but was only so in retaliation. Even so, he needed great self-discipline as well as a happy disposition to keep him, in 1733 and in 1741, from feeling aggrieved and showing bitterness. Luckily, he had this too. Honest Shippen's respect for Walpole is often quoted to demonstrate Walpole's knack of not turning his political enemies into personal enemies. Speaker Onslow, whose temperament was not at all like Walpole's, and who was indeed accused by Horace Walpole of favouring the opposition, may be quoted to show Walpole's equally important talent for not turning his colleagues against him.

He was a wise and able minister, and the best man from the goodness of his heart, which was characteristic in him, to live with and live under of any great man I ever knew. . . . On his retirement from office, his retreat was entire from the concerns of government, but not from the following estimation of almost every man of those that had surrounded him when in the height of power.

Later in the century, Walpole's reputation was maintained, and enhanced, by the tributes that his successors paid to him. His reputation for skill in public finance dated from his first period as First Lord of the Treasury in 1716: it was high and remained high. Pelham was taught by him, and the two First Lords most renowned for financial competence, North and the younger Pitt, acknowledged his mastery. Statesmen were joined by economists: Josiah Tucker called him 'the best commercial minister this country ever produced', while Chalmers and Adam Smith praised his commercial and colonial policy. In the 1750s, the elder Pitt rejoiced that he had been 'at peace' with Walpole, 'that very able minister', before he died. Pitt also repented his opposition to the Excise Bill and 'owned he was for an Inland Duty, and a Free Port, that everybody must know by Inland Duties he meant Excise. . . . That Sir Rob. Walpole meant honestly in the Excise Scheme'.

This confession on Pitt's part is often quoted as testimony to his honesty. It is at least equally apt as testimony to the dishonesty of the opposition to Walpole. Burke castigated the chauvinistic public opinion that forced Walpole into a shameful privateering war in 1739, the intrigues and cabals that brought about his fall, and the false picture of him circulated by those who were jealous of his position.

Mr. Walpole [Burke declared in 1791] was an honourable man and a sound Whig. He was not, as the Jacobites and discontented Whigs of his

> time have represented him, and as ill-informed people still represent him, a prodigal and corrupt minister. They charged him, in their libels and seditious conversations, with having first reduced corruption to a system. Such was their cant. But he was far from governing by corruption. He governed by party attachments. . . . With many virtues, publick and private, he had his faults; but his faults were superficial. . . . The prudence, steadiness and vigilance of that man, joined to the greatest possible lenity in his character and his politicks, preserved the crown to this royal family, and with it, their laws and liberties to this country.

This is appreciation of Walpole's policy and character by his contemporaries and the next generation or so. Appreciation of his constitutional achievement could hardly come until later. Even the novelty of a first minister in the House of Commons was not generally applauded by Walpole's contemporaries, nor seen as an increase in Commons power. Rather, it was regarded as a threat to the Commons' independence. Nevertheless, even in the eighteenth century, there was some understanding, as well as very vocal criticism, of the new kind of political practice that Walpole worked to establish. Not all who valued the 'independence' of the House of Commons thought it was to be obtained by abolishing placemen and long parliaments. Speaker Onslow believed it had been obtained by the Septennial Act, which began the 'era of independence of the House of Commons from their former dependence' on King and Lords. David Hume argued that the power of the House of Commons was potentially so great that crown influence – placemen in the Commons – served the useful purpose of counteracting it.

> We may therefore give to this influence what name we please; we may call it by the invidious appellations of *corruption* and *dependence*; but some degree and some kind of it are inseparable from the very nature of the constitution, and necessary to the preservation of our mixed government.

In a way, Hume's view was an old-fashioned one. It saw the constitution in terms of three powers, three associated and hostile parts, King, Lords, and Commons, each of which must be prevented from overwhelming the others. A more forward-looking and perhaps more perceptive view would see placemen in the Commons as a positive advantage to the Commons, not just a necessary diminution of the Commons' excessive power. Of course, one would not expect to find this view often, in a period which had only just achieved this balance of power, and felt it precarious. It is, however, to be found occasionally. One instance is Bishop Sherlock's insistence in 1731 that dependency, not independency, was the right relationship for the three parts of parliament. Another is George Selwyn's plea in 1740 that the exclusion of placemen 'would lessen that Regard which the Crown now finds it necessary to show to you' and that the 'Correspondence and Connexion between the Crown and Parliament' which placemen symbolized was necessary to constitutional tranquillity. Nevertheless, in general, concern for the balance of power and for independence in Bolingbroke's sense, not Onslow's, overrode any thoughts like these.

Criticism therefore concentrated, as it has done ever since, on Walpole's methods rather than on the purpose they served. This was more than half self-defeating. Many advocates of Place Bills and of short parliaments did not see, or did not appear to see, that these things implied an alternative conception of government, and a new one. To ask for annual or even short parliaments in the eighteenth century could not simply be a request to return to the past. As Willes said in 1734, it was all very well to talk about 'our ancient Constitution; but it has been so often varied and altered, that it will be found difficult to fix upon a Time when it was such as we ought or would desire to return to . . . we are surely not to take the Time when our Constitution was weak and in its Infancy?'

Whatever form annual parliaments took, it could not be a fourteenth-century form. Either they would have prevented executive action altogether, which was absurd, or they would have been simply assenting bodies, without any power of initiative. Place Bills, too, would have separated the government from the House of Commons at the very time that the Commons had gained control over policy.

Of course, it would not have been impossible to put these things into practice – it is, however, not easy to see what the practice would have been like, and the advocates of Place Bills and short parliaments do not help. They talked of 'independence' and 'corruption', of 'freedom' and 'influence', but there they stopped. Some indeed took the view that there was no need for connection between the government and the House of Commons because a 'good' House of Commons would always support a 'good' government, or, as Pulteney put it in 1740, if there were no placemen in the Commons 'The Publick Good would then be the only Aim of Ministers, as well as Members'. This is a very rosy conception of government. For want of a better name, it may be called 'extra-parliamentary government'. It might have turned out to be something like enlightened despotism, a form of government much discussed and sometimes practised in eighteenth-century Europe. Perhaps this is another name for government by a patriot King.

Real appreciation of Walpole's constitutional achievement came later, at the time of the passing of the 1832 Reform Bill, and even more in the generation or so after it. This was because he was then seen as the first practitioner of 'parliamentary government', which was defined as a constitution in which the powers of the crown are exercised by ministers who are members of parliament, and guide its proceedings and hold office only while they have parliament's confidence. Walpole's constitutional achievement was perhaps a little distorted by this limelight, but at least it focussed attention for the first time on its greatness and its innovatory character.

The great argument about the effect of parliamentary reform on the constitution holds unexpected echoes of the argument between Walpole and Bolingbroke a hundred years before, about the meaning of the balance of the constitution – interdependence *versus* independence. It was still widely assumed in 1832 that the constitutional balance established in 1689 existed in practice, as well as being desirable in theory. Indeed, the Reform Bill debates are very much concerned with this theme, the reformers arguing that reform would not upset the balance, their opponents that it would, and that this was the basic objection to reform. The muddle arose because of the two descriptions of the constitution: the old description, 'balance', and the new description, 'parliamentary government'. What is the relationship between them?

The simple answer in the mid-nineteenth century was that balance was an outmoded theory, which did not fit the facts. It should be replaced by parliamentary government, which did. J. J. Park said this in 1832, just before the first Reform Bill. It was repeated in 1867, just before the second Reform Bill, by Alpheus Todd, whose two volumes on the British constitution are entitled *Parliamentary Government*. Todd wrote of the wide discrepancy between the theory of the constitution (balance) and the practice of the constitution (parliamentary government). Parliamentary government, he said, had been the practice of the constitution since Walpole's time. Park was a professor of law and Todd an official of the Canadian House of Commons; between them in time came the third Earl Grey, a politician. Like them, he argued that the common description of the British constitution had ceased to be correct since the establishment of parliamentary government. Parliamentary government began 'very imperfectly' in William III's reign and was 'completely established' under Walpole.

Yet, having made this case for a new theory of the constitution, which would stretch back to Walpole, both Todd and Grey confuse the issue, and their readers. Todd does so by implying that balance and parliamentary government co-exist. The Reform Bill, he says, has made parliamentary government more difficult, but so far 'the balance of the Constitution, though jeopardized, has not been overthrown.' Grey states that 'the balance of the Constitution' was in danger of being destroyed in the 1850s because of the 'too great diminution' of the government's influence in parliament.

The balance of the constitution cannot, at the same time, be both an out-of-date theory and in danger of being destroyed. No one solved this muddle. The answer is that the theory was perhaps getting out-of-date in the middle of the nineteenth century, but that it was not yet out-of-date in Walpole's time. The error is to think that Walpole's constitution was the same as the mid-nineteenth-century constitution, and that 'parliamentary government' describes both, and therefore that the theory of balance was discrepant with practice from the beginning. All this is wrong, because the premise is wrong. Grey's description of mid-nineteenth-century parliamentary government does not fit the Walpolian state of affairs. 'The executive power and the power of legislation', Grey wrote, 'are virtually united in the same hands.' This was not true in Walpole's time. In fact, I doubt whether it was quite true in Grey's, or indeed in any period until the House of Commons and the government were chosen at the same time and therefore had the same colour.

In Walpole's time there was no 'cabinet' which one can call the 'executive power'. There was a group of ministers chosen by the King, usually individually and at separate times. Ministers and the House of Commons were chosen by different agents – ministers by the King, and the Commons by the electorate – as well as at different times. Walpole owed his position to the King, even if the King happened to be more aware than some of his successors of the convenience of having as first minister a man pre-eminent in the Commons. He owed his continuance in office to the King's continued favour, to his own continued ascendancy in the Commons, and to his withdrawal of unpopular measures. 'Balance' may have been incompatible with mid-nineteenth-century parliamentary government, but it was compatible with Walpole's position and had not, in 1867, been out-of-date for 150 years.

One of the shrewdest commentators on Walpole's achievement was Peel, one of the 'great practical politicians' who, to quote Lecky in 1877, 'have usually estimated him [Walpole] far more highly than men of letters'. Peel wrote no books on the constitution, yet saw all politics through constitutional spectacles. It is significant that he praised Walpole without mentioning 'the cabinet' or 'the executive power'. He praised him, that is, almost as a contemporary might have done – as a King's minister. Philip Stanhope, later fifth Earl Stanhope, who was writing a history of George I's reign, asked Peel for his comments. Peel found the subject 'so attractive' that he had to restrain himself from writing 'a pamphlet instead of a letter'. Stanhope was the great-great-grandson of the Stanhope who ousted Walpole in 1717. Perhaps ancestral piety forbade him to admire Walpole. But he was foolish to compare Walpole unfavourably with the heroic and romantic Strafford, abandoned by Charles I and put to death at the beginning of the Civil War. So Peel wrote, in December 1833:

> No doubt the qualities displayed in the time of fierce civil contention, – in the revolution of opinions and forms of government, are much more interesting, much more captivating in description, than the qualities by which a new dynasty is to be gradually confirmed, and by which peace at home and abroad is to be secured. . . .
>
> Try Walpole and Strafford by the *result* of their counsels, by their result to the Monarchs whom they served, and how powerful would the contrast be in favour of Walpole! . . . Lips compressed in iron resolution,

and glances of fire, are very becoming to a hero; they suit the iron times in which Strafford lived; but why not let Walpole 'laugh the heart's laugh, and nod the approving head', if the heart's laugh was not out of place, and if, in spite of his enemies, he kept a head wherewith to nod his approbation?

Peel's quotation is taken from a poem written by Charles Hanbury Williams in 1742, which Coxe, Walpole's first biographer, sourly calls 'a portrait . . . though it contains more truth than poetry'. Here are another two short extracts from it:

> Thus was he form'd to govern, and to please;
> Familiar greatness, dignity with ease,
> Compos'd his frame, admired in ev'ry state,
> In private amiable, in public great;
> . . . .
> Whose knowledge, courage, temper, all surpris'd,
> Whom many lov'd, few hated, none despis'd.

Walpole was a curiously private man: this indeed is one of his attractions. His public achievements can be seen, and his opinions about public matters and politics are there for everyone to read. But his personal emotions and feelings – whether he was happy, moved, hurt – were rarely expressed. He was a peculiarly self-disciplined man and, at the same time, not an egotistical one. He was self-contained, self-sufficient, and perhaps made more so by circumstances.

Thus his personal qualities are more easily perceived than his feelings. There is indeed no lack of testimony to his personal qualities, both in public and in private life. Good temper and generosity of mind are the two qualities most insisted on, by friends and opponents alike. Chesterfield, an opponent, described Walpole as 'not vindictive, but on the contrary very placable to those who had injured him the most'. Pulteney, perhaps exonerating himself from vindictiveness, thought Walpole 'of a temper so calm and equal, and so hard to be provoked, that he was very sure he [Walpole] never felt the bitterest invectives against him for half an hour'. Governor Pownall, a thoughtful appraiser, gave a similar verdict:

> Although he acquired a high degree of power, and possessed a degree of influence which would have enabled him as a man to do anything; yet, even under provocation that can exasperate, *he never did an injury*, scarce ever revenged one. He had a magnanimity above all the resentments of the private man.

Walpole himself may be quoted. His rejoinder to Pulteney's diatribes in February 1734 is one of the best examples, but a typical one, of his good temper and refusal to be drawn into a slanging match. For this, a very high degree of what Hervey called Walpole's 'steadiness of temper' was required. 'Most of what the gentleman [Pulteney] said seemed in a particular manner to be directed at me, which indeed is a subject I always speak of with the greatest unwillingness, as it is very little worth the attention of the House'. Again, in the Place Bill debate of January 1740, Walpole refused to be angered either by Sandys's talk of 'the Encroachments of an ambitious Prince, or guilty Minister' or by Pulteney's picture of a duped and enslaved House of Commons. 'When I look around me', Walpole said, 'I must look upon the Danger, now pretended to be so real and imminent, to be as chimerical a Danger as the most luxuriant Fancy can invent.' He added a piece of the cool good-natured wisdom of which none of his opponents was capable:

> In all Questions, Sir, which do not admit of Demonstration, there must be a Variety of Opinions; and as Questions of a political Nature are less capable of Demonstration than any other, it is natural to see a Difference of Sentiments in every Country like this, where the People

have not only a Power to judge, but a Liberty to talk and write against the Measures pursued by the Government . . . all those who disapprove of the Measures of the Government conclude, that the Approbation of those that differ from them, proceeds from the Influence of some lucrative Post they are in Possession or Expectation of; and on the other hand, those that approve of, and support the Measures pursued by the Government, are apt to conclude, that the Opposition is entirely owing to Party-Prejudice, or to Malice and Resentment. For my Part, I shall always endeavour to keep in the middle Course, and to believe that both are in the wrong.

There are many tributes to the same 'most amiable and benevolent qualities' in private life. 'Never' [said Egmont, another critic] 'was a man in private life more beloved, and his enemies allow, no man did ever in private life deserve it more.' One of the most attractive tributes is a poem written by Lady Mary Wortley Montagu on seeing a portrait of Walpole as a young man.

These were the lively eyes and rosy hue
Of Robin's face when Robin first I knew;
The gay companion and the favourite guest,
Loved without awe, and without views caressed.
His cheerful smile and honest open look
Added new graces to the truths he spoke.
Then every man found something to commend,
The pleasant neighbour and the worthy friend;
The gen'rous master of a private house,
The tender father and indulgent spouse.
The hardest censors, at the worst, believed
His temper was too easily deceived:
A consequential ill good nature draws;
A bad effect but from a noble cause.

This may be matched by Pope – Bolingbroke's friend and therefore certainly Walpole's enemy – who was 'at last' persuaded to go and see Sir Robert:

Seen him I have, but in his happier hour
Of social pleasure, ill-exchanged for power;
Seen him, uncumber'd with the venal tribe,
Smile without art, and win without a bribe.

Walpole's tastes, again, are known by what he did, seldom by what he said or wrote. He clearly delighted in active country pursuits and in building. He rode and hunted regularly whether he was in Norfolk or in London. Like other heads of eighteenth-century country families, he pulled down his old family house and replaced it with a grander and more convenient one built in a modified Palladian style, surrounding it with a park and handsome plantations. In London, he was responsible for building the new Treasury Chambers and for the conversion of 10 Downing Street into an official residence. He was a keen and knowledgeable botanist and searched for rare and exotic plants for his gardens, which he planned, before the building of the house began, with the well-known gardener Charles Bridgeman. They were one of the earliest examples of an approach to the art of landscape gardening later perfected by Kent – the creation of a picture, a house in a natural setting.

The contents of his house provided incontrovertible evidence of his fine and discriminating taste. It was furnished with exact judgement and sense of fitness; it was embellished with magnificent statuary, busts and urns; and, above all, it contained a superb collection of pictures, probably the best in England, including a wealth of Old Masters – Rembrandts, Titians, Poussins, Rubenses, Raphaels – many of which Walpole justly rated more highly than his son Horace did. Walpole collected his pictures over a very long period, beginning at least as early as 1715. Some were bought in sales at home, some were presented to him, some commissioned – the Kneller portraits of him and his first wife, for example; some were bought, on his directions, abroad – in France, Holland

and Italy – by friends, ambassadors, his brother Horatio and his sons. Some of the best were hung at 10 Downing Street and in his rooms in the new Treasury; these he brought to Houghton when he retired.

For, in 1742, Walpole's intention was to retire, not just to resign, and to live a country and not a town life. So he lived at Houghton and lodged, when he had to go to London, in Arlington Street. It was the first time he had been free from official commitments since Houghton was planned in 1722. A letter he wrote from Houghton in 1743 is one of the few in which he did express his feelings, or at any rate imply his pleasures. It was probably written to General Charles Churchill, whose son later married Mary, Walpole's daughter by Maria Skerrett. Its style is gentle and whimsical, and the letter was later converted into a Latin ode by Nicholas Hardinge, the scholarly Clerk of the House of Commons.

> This place [he wrote] affords no news, no subject of amusement and entertainment to you fine Gentlemen. Men of wit and pleasure about town understand not the language, nor taste the charms of the inanimate world: my flatterers here are all mutes, the Oaks the Beeches and the Chesnuts seem to contend, which shall best please the Lord of the Mannor: They cannot deceive, they will not lie. . . . Within doors we come a little nearer to real life and admire upon the almost speaking Canvas, all the airs and graces which the proudest of town ladies can boast, with these I am satisfied as they gratify me with all I wish and all I want, and expect nothing in return which I am not able to give. If these, dear Charles, are any temptations, I heartily invite you to come and partake of them!

So two of Walpole's pleasures – pictures and the countryside – are combined, in a picture painted by himself. He is in it himself, smiling at himself, but in the background, not dominating the picture.

This ability to smile at himself is seen in his relations with his youngest son Horace, who was twenty-five when Walpole retired. Horace's sophisticated tastes excluded country pastimes. He was by choice a town dweller and, as Hanbury Williams wrote a few years later:

> My young Walpole, blest with truest taste,
> Adorn'd with learning, with politeness grac'd.

So, in inviting Horace to Houghton, and implying affection and pleasure in Horace's company, Walpole absolved him from any obligation or sense of duty. Walpole's bantering tone is perhaps a protection against the possibility of rebuff. For example, he wrote to Horace in July 1744:

> All the disagreeable symptoms I had, are gone, and this I verily believe will make you partake in my pleasures, I know what would add to them when you can persuade y^r^self to sacrifice the Joys of the *Beau-monde* to ye amusements of a dull rural life.
>
> But we all love to please our selves, and may it allways be in y^r^ power to make y^r^self as happy as I wish you.

There was no rebuff. In these years of Walpole's retirement, Horace spent much time at Houghton. He composed his *Sermon on Painting* there, in 1742, and *Patapan*, a skit on politicians, in 1743; and, of course, he wrote letters. He hobnobbed with Vertue, since 1722 a frequent visitor to Walpole and his pictures both at Houghton and in London. In July 1743, Horace finished *Aedes Walpolianae*, his catalogue and comments on the pictures, and dedicated it to his father. More surprisingly, Horace is found riding, coursing, and even planning to hunt.

Horace Walpole had a deep and lifelong affection for his father. It was not based only on filial duty and respect for his father's concrete political achievements, but on appreciation of his character and tastes. They had more tastes in common than is often realized: pictures and gardening are two of them. If Horace had been the eldest son, he would have inherited Walpole's pictures and works of art. Walpole – as well as Horace – would then have been renowned as a connoisseur and dilettante and no one would have called him a 'typical Norfolk squire'. He paid enormous sums for his pictures and for the building and decoration of his house, and – after spending on them the gains from his South Sea investments – he borrowed. He died leaving large debts. As it turned out, his eldest son Robert did not live at Houghton, and died only six years after his father. Robert's only son George, the third Earl, was a weak and erratic spendthrift. In 1779 he sold the pictures to Catherine the Great of Russia for £36,000.

When, therefore, Horace succeeded as fourth Earl in 1791, at the age of seventy-four, the house and estate were ruined and the pictures gone. Most of them are still in the Hermitage in Leningrad. Horace Walpole described the sale as 'the most signal mortification to my idolatry for my father's memory, that it could receive. It is stripping the temple of his glory and of his affection.' The fact that Horace did not inherit the pictures his father and he both loved is a sad loss for us as well as for him, for it has certainly affected people's assessment of the kind of man Walpole was. It is sad, too, that Horace refused to write – despite his consciousness that he had much to tell posterity – a biography of his father. Biography in the ordinary sense was too pedestrian a task for this versatile and voluminous chronicler of his times, but how valuable to posterity an impressionistic sketch by him would have been. Even in refusing, however, Horace measured himself against his father. 'I have none of his matchless wisdom, or unsullied virtues, or heroic firmness', he wrote.

Walpole had been ill just before his last session in the House of Commons. He was seriously and painfully ill in the winter of 1744, but travelled to London because the King had asked his advice. He died there, on 18 March 1745, in his Arlington Street house. He was buried at Houghton, 'the world allowing him to be the only man in England fit to be what he has been'. No epitaph was written on his grave.

A NOTE ON BOOKS

Reports of Walpole's speeches, read alongside those of his supporters and opponents, form an excellent introduction to the man. Two contemporary collections of reports on parliamentary debates are of particular interest here: Richard Chandler, *History and Proceedings of the House of Commons from the Restoration to the Present Time*, 14 vols (1742–4) and Ebenezer Timberland, *History and Proceedings of the House of Lords* (1742–3). For Walpole's speeches, Chandler is in some instances fuller and in others less full than William Coxe, *Memoirs of the Life and Administration of Sir Robert Walpole* (1798). This, the first biography of Walpole, is a comprehensive work of great scholarship. It remains of immense value for Coxe's extensive publication of original material, much of which is now lost. Coxe's *Memoirs of Horatio Walpole* (1802) is also useful.

Walpole's pamphlets, like his speeches, are vigorous and informative. Amongst pamphlets written by his opponents, Pulteney's are the best ones to read – for instance *An Enquiry into the Conduct of our Domestick Affairs, from the year 1721* (1734). Selections from *The Craftsman* can conveniently be read in *Lord Bolingbroke: Political Writings*, edited by I. Kramnick (1972). The *London Journal* or the *Free Briton* (both pro-Walpole) should be looked at too. Hardwicke's *Walpoliana* (1783) contains anecdotes of Walpole.

John, Lord Hervey (*Some Materials towards Memoirs of the reign of George II*) is a waspish supporter. Some of Horace Walpole's letters are worth reading. A tiny selection of them can be found in the Everyman Library (ed. W. Hadley). James Ralph, *A Critical History of the Administration of Sir Robert Walpole* (1743), quotes from contemporary material. Edmund Burke, *Appeal from the New to the Old Whigs* (1791) is important for his view of Walpole's contribution to Whig doctrine.

Just as nearly everything written in the second quarter of the eighteenth century mentions Walpole, so he has a place in all modern books on the eighteenth century. But, since Coxe, there has been a dearth of biographies. The few nineteenth-century ones are not useful, though some references to him are of course interesting historiographically. Peel's comments, some of which are quoted in Norman Gash, *Life of Sir Robert Peel* (1972), go deeper than this. There is also a strange lack of modern biographies of Walpole's colleagues – and, indeed, of his opponents too, except for Bolingbroke. Although J. H. Plumb, *Sir Robert Walpole* (2 vols, 1956 and 1960) unfortunately stops at 1734, it contains both a survey of 'Walpole's world' and an appraisal of Walpole. Until the third volume appears, its absence underlines Mr Plumb's deliberate emphasis on Walpole's early career – a valuable corrective to the usual concentration on the years after 1721, which almost implies that Walpole then sprang from nowhere into being 'Prime Minister'.

For some discussion of the background of Walpole's problems and achievement the reader may consult: J. H. Plumb, *The Growth of Stability 1675–1725* (1967), Betty Kemp, *King and Commons 1660–1832* (1957), and John B. Owen, *The Rise of the Pelhams* (1957); D. B. Horn, *Britain and Europe in the Eighteenth Century* (1967) and Basil Williams, *Stanhope* (1932) and *Carteret and Newcastle* (1943); T. S. Ashton, *Economic Fluctuations in England 1700–*

1800 (1959), A. C. Carter, *The English Public Debt in the Eighteenth Century* (1968) and P. G. M. Dickson, *The Financial Revolution in England* (1967). For the opposition to Walpole C. B. Realey, *The Early Opposition to Walpole 1720–27* (1931) and P. Vaucher, *La Crise du Ministère Walpole 1733–34* (1924) may be singled out. *Essays in Eighteenth-Century History*, edited by Rosalind Mitchison (1966) reprints articles by G. C. Gibbs on Walpole's foreign policy and by E. R. Turner on the excise scheme.

I select the following as illuminating on particular aspects of Walpole's England: G. A. Cranfield, *The Development of the Provincial Newspaper 1700–1760* (1962); M. D. George, *English Political Caricature*, vol. 1 (1959); L. Hanson, *The Government and the Press 1695–1763* (1936); I. Kramnick, *Bolingbroke and his Circle* (1968); J. M. Beattie, *The English Court in the Reign of George I* (1967); Geoffrey Holmes, *The Trial of Dr Sacheverell* (1974); R. W. Ketton-Cremer, *Life of Horace Walpole* (1940); M. Jourdain, *The Work of William Kent* (1948).

Two books – Reed Browning, *The Duke of Newcastle* (1975) and Paul Langford, *The Excise Crisis* (1975) – were published too late for me to read before *Sir Robert Walpole* was prepared.

INDEX